THE ARMENIAN COOKBOOK

THE ARMENIAN COOKBOOK

BY RACHEL HOGROGIAN

ILLUSTRATED BY NONNY HOGROGIAN

ATHENEUM / NEW YORK / 1983

For the Hogrogians, the Ansoorians, the Boyajians, the Tashjians, the Manoukians, the Vartenissians, the Kherdians and for all their "ians" to come

Armenian food is as varied as the Near East and the areas the Armenians came from. There is midia dolma (stuffed mussels), a specialty from Constantinople; keshkeg and pacha, the hearty meals eaten in the mountains around Erzinjan; and lahmajoon, a meat pie that is very special when made by the people of Aintab.

There is a natural overlapping with Turkish, Greek, Persian and Arabic foods. Although the Armenians like to think they originated all of the favorites such as shish kebab, kufta, pilaf and pakhlava, it is not always clear where these originated, but it is certain that the Armenians refined recipes and added subtleties of flavors as only they could.

Pari Akhorjhag (*Bon Appetit*)!

I would like to thank all my friends and relatives for their many hours of testing, tasting, and recipe exchanging. This book would not have been possible without their support.

CONTENTS

abour	soup
adjeh	a parsley omelet usually served as an Easter appetizer
Ajem pilaf	Persian pilaf
anoush	sweet
anoushabour	traditional New Year pudding
anousheghen	sweets or desserts
baba ghanoush	eggplant salad
baki	Lenten
bamiya	okra
banir	cheese
bastegh	grape juice and cornstarch dried on a flat surface (sometimes referred to as shoeleather)
biberr	pepper
bishi	pancakes, Armenian style
boerag	a many-layered pastry with a filling; occasionally a vegetable with a filling
boombar	stuffed lamb casings
bourma	rolled, shirred strudel pastry with syrup and a nut filling
bulghour	cracked wheat which can be bought fine, medium, or large in Armenian or Greek grocery stores
bulghourov spanakh	spinach with bulghour
chi kufta	Armenian-style steak tartare
choereg	a lightly sweetened breakfast bun
dabgadz	fried

derev	leaves, usually referring to grape leaves which are used in Armenian cooking
derev dolma	stuffed grape leaves
dolma	a stuffed food, most often a vegetable stuffed with meat and/or rice
Donn orva pilaf	Holiday pilaf
duezmah	a casserole made with eggplant and meat
dutmaj abour	soup made with yoghurt and noodles
ekmek kadayif	a syrupy dessert served with a topping of thick cream
enguinar	artichokes
erishtah abour	noodle soup
fassoulia	beans
feeshneyov anoush	sour cherry preserve
filo	prepared strudel-like dough available in Near Eastern specialty grocery shops
gatnabour	rice pudding
gelorig	meat-ball soup
geragoornerr	stew-type meals usually made with meat and vegetables
gorgod	a grain like barley but larger
guevej	a baked stew
halvah	a sweet paste candy or dessert
hav	chicken
havgit	egg
havgitov fassoulia	string beans with eggs
hummos	chick-pea dip

imam bayeldi	a baked eggplant dish
imrig halvah	a pudding made of Cream of Wheat and pine nuts
Izmir kufta	hamburgers as they were made in Smyrna
jajukh	cucumbers and yoghurt
jevisli	walnut-filled cookies
jezveh	Turkish coffeepot usually made of brass, with a long handle
jigerr	liver
kadayif	a pastry of shredded dough with a nut filling and syrup; sometimes cheese is substituted for the nut filling
karabich	nut-filled cookies made with semolina and whiskey
katah	a flaky breakfast pastry
keshkeg	lamb and gorgod cooked to the consistency of oatmeal
khabourga	roast lamb stuffed with fancy pilaf
khaimakh	a thick cream topping served on desserts such as ekmek kadayif
khavourma	braised lamb
kheyma	most often refers to a ground meat mixture, but sometimes refers to other mixtures to be used as stuffings
khoritzov katah	a flaky breakfast pastry with a buttery filling
khoshop	a sour cherry drink
khourabia	Armenian shortbread
khumoreghen	pastry

khundsor	apple
khundsorov dolma	stuffed baked apples
kimion	cumin
kimionov kufta	meat balls flavored with cumin
kouzou kzartma	baked shoulder of lamb with sliced potatoes
kufta	chopped meat often shaped into patties or meat balls with stuffing
lahana	cabbage
lahmajoon	Armenian meat pies
lavash	flat bread
lehzoo	tongue
lokhma	a creampuff-type dessert
lule kebab	baked lamburgers
madzoon	the Armenian name for yoghurt
madzoonov	with madzoon
madzoonabourov kufta	meat balls served in soup made with madzoon
mahleb	a ground seed used in pastries available in specialty grocery shops
mamoul	a nut-filled cookie sprinkled with confectioner's sugar
mamounya	a nut-filled cookie dipped in syrup
manti	meat-filled pastry boats baked with broth and served with madzoon
mees	meat
meeseghen	meat dishes
meesov geragoornerr	stew-like meals made with meat
meza	appetizer
midia	mussels

midia dolma	stuffed mussels
moussaka	eggplant and lamb casserole
muedjatdera	bulghour cooked with lentils
muhallabi	pudding made with rice flour
naatiffe	a marshmallow frosting made with orange water
noush	almonds
noushov pilaf	a rice dish made with almonds
ooghegh	brains
pacha	stewed lamb tongues and calves' feet
paghlah	fava beans
pakhlava	a flaky, many-layered nut-filled pastry
panchareghen	vegetables
pandjarabour	Swiss chard stew
pasterma	dried beef seasoned with fenugreek (called chaimen in Armenian)
patlijan	eggplant
patlijan karni yarek	baked stuffed eggplant
patlijanov	with eggplant
piaz	salad made with beans
pideh	Armenian bread made in a round loaf
pilaf	steamed rice or bulghour
plaki	stew made with dry white beans
porov	with stuffing
prinz	rice
prinzov pilaf	pilaf made with rice
raki	alcoholic beverage of Armenia made with raisins and flavored with anise
rechel	a candy-like preserve made with pumpkin

revani	farina nut cake soaked in syrup
salata	salad
shish	skewer
shish kebab	skewered barbequed lamb
shishboereg	a hearty soup filled with dumplings, croutons, and chick peas
simit	a crisp breakfast pastry
sini kufta	baked chopped lamb and bulghour with an exotic filling
sokh	onions
sokhov dolma	stuffed onions
soorj	Armenian coffee
soudjookh	Armenian sausage, highly spiced
spanakh	spinach
susam	sesame seeds
susamov khumoreghen	pastries with sesame seeds
taheen	sesame paste
tan	a summer beverage made with madzoon and water
tarama	a dip made with carp roe
tass kebab	potted lamb
tomates	tomato
tomatesov	with tomatoes
topik	a Lenten dish made with chick peas, onions, and sesame paste
tourshi	pickles
tsoug	fish
tsougov plaki	baked fish (red snapper) dressed with stewed vegetables

turlu guevej	a baked lamb dish with a mixture of vegetables
tutum	squash, pumpkin, or zucchini
tutumov rechel	pumpkin preserve
ungouyz	walnuts
ungouyzov khumoreghen	walnut pastry
vosp	lentil
vospov kheyma	lentil patties made with bulghour and onions
yalanchi dolma	grape leaves with a rice stuffing
yerigamoonk	kidneys
yevaylen	and so on

MEZAS (APPETIZERS)

TOURSHI / *Mixed pickles*

2 quarts

4 carrots	*½ pound string beans*
1 small head cauliflower	*2 cloves garlic*
4 stalks celery	*4 sprigs fresh dill*

Wash and scrape the carrots. Cut them lengthwise into quarters, and again into 4-inch pieces. Wash the cauliflower and separate into small flowerettes. Wash the celery, remove the leaves, and cut into 4-inch pieces. Wash the string beans, and snap off both ends of the bean. Peel the cloves of garlic, and wash the dill.

Sterilize two quart jars in boiling water. Pack the jars with the prepared vegetables. Add 1 clove of garlic and 2 sprigs of dill to each jar. Be sure to pack the jars as tightly as possible, and place a jar ring around the neck of the jar.

BRINE

1 quart water	*¼ cup salt*
1 cup cider vinegar	*1 tablespoon sugar*

Combine the water, vinegar, salt, and sugar in a saucepan. Bring the mixture to a boil and pour enough of the hot brine into the jars to overflow. Seal the jars as tightly as possible. The pickles will be ready to serve in 2 to 4 weeks, depending on how tart you like them. The longer you leave them, the tarter they will get.

BOERAG I / *A delicious flaky pastry with a mild cheese filling*
40 small pastries

FILLING

1¾ pounds muenster cheese	½ cup finely chopped parsley
¼ teaspoon salt	3 eggs

Grate the cheese into a mixing bowl. Add the other ingredients, mix well, and set aside while you prepare the dough.

PASTRY

4 cups flour	1 cup warm water
1 teaspoon salt	4 tablespoons melted butter
1 heaping tablespoon baking powder	1 pound sweet butter, melted
2 eggs	1 beaten egg

Mix the flour, salt, and baking powder in a warm mixing bowl. In another bowl combine the 2 eggs, water, and 4 tablespoons of butter. Make a well in the dry ingredients and pour into it the combined liquids. Mix by hand, then knead the dough for about 5 minutes or until the ingredients are thoroughly blended.

Wet a towel with warm water and wring dry. Cover the dough with the towel and let it rest for 10 minutes. Knead the dough for another 5 minutes, then roll it into the shape of a long loaf. Cut it into 10 pieces. Knead each piece into a flattened ball. Sprinkle the dough with flour to keep the pieces from sticking to each other. Cover the dough again and let it rest for 15 minutes.

Sprinkle a rolling pin lightly with flour. Take one piece of dough and roll it out to a diameter of 15 inches. Brush the surface generously with melted butter. Then take the next piece of dough, roll it out to the same width, place it over the first layer and coat it generously with butter. Continue this step until all of the dough has been rolled out, stacked, and buttered. Fold the stack of sheets in half (like a half moon) and refrigerate for 25 to 30 minutes. Then cut the dough into 10 strips in one direction and 4 in the other (to make about 40 squares). Store the pieces in the refrigerator to keep the butter solid. Remove them one at a time as needed.

Before filling, roll each piece into a 4-inch square. Put 1 heaping teaspoon of filling in the center of the square. Fold the dough diagonally in half to make a triangular shape and pinch the edges together to seal.

Place the boerags on a buttered baking pan, brush the tops with a beaten egg, and bake them at 350° F. for 30 or 35 minutes until golden brown.

VARIATION FILLING

2 *large onions, finely chopped*
2 *tablespoons butter*
1 *pound chopped lamb*
salt and pepper to taste

⅛ *teaspoon allspice*
⅛ *teaspoon cinnamon*
⅓ *cup parsley, finely chopped*
¼ *cup pine nuts*

Sauté the onions in butter. Add the chopped lamb and seasonings and continue cooking until the onions are soft and the meat has browned. Add the parsley and pine nuts.

There are probably as many filling variations as there are Armenian chefs, but these two are my favorites.

BOERAG II / *This boerag is a delicious, simple-to-prepare, cheese-filled pastry. It is made with strudel-like pastry sheets, which are sold in one-pound packages. One package will make about 75 cocktail-sized boerags. They can be made in advance and frozen. Brush the surface with melted butter before freezing. They can be baked as needed by placing the frozen boerags in the oven a half hour before serving.*

75 small pastries

CHEESE FILLING

2 *pounds muenster cheese,*   4 *egg*s
     grated   ½ *cup parsley, finely chopped*

Combine the ingredients in a mixing bowl. Mix well, and set aside while you prepare the pastry.

PASTRY

1 pound filo   *1 pound sweet butter, melted*

Place the sheets of pastry on the table and cover them with a towel to prevent the sheets from drying out. Take one sheet of dough at a time and cover the balance. Place the sheet of dough on the table. Brush the entire surface with melted butter, using a pastry brush. Place another sheet of dough directly over the first sheet. Cut the double sheet into 4 strips lengthwise with a knife. Each strip will be about 2 × 10 inches. Place a teaspoonful of the filling on one end of the strip. Fold a corner of the sheet over the filling into a triangle. Continue folding to the end of the strip, and you will have a triangular-shaped boerag. Make the balance of the boerags and arrange them on a baking sheet. Brush the top of each boerag with melted butter. Bake in a 375° F. oven for 25 to 30 minutes. Serve them with cocktails while they are warm.

OOGHEGH / *Brain salad*

4 servings

1 *pound lamb brains*
lettuce
salt and pepper to taste
½ *cup chopped parsley*

½ *cup chopped scallions*
optional: *lemon juice*
    olive oil

Wash the brains thoroughly in cold water and remove the loose red veins. Place the brains in a saucepan, fill it with water to cover them, and season the water with salt. Bring the water to a boil and simmer the brains for 10 minutes. Drain and chill the brains. Cut them into thick slices and arrange them on a bed of lettuce leaves. Sprinkle the brains with salt and pepper and garnish them with the parsley and scallions.

I prefer this dish plain, but many Armenians serve it with a dressing of lemon juice and olive oil.

LEHZOO / *Lamb tongue*

4 servings

1 *pound lamb tongues*
salt and pepper to taste

½ *cup chopped parsley*
½ *cup chopped scallions*

Wash the lamb tongues in cold water. Trim away all of the fat and gristle from the back end of each tongue. Place the tongues in a saucepan, fill it with cold water to cover the tongues, and season it with salt. Simmer the tongues until they are tender. Drain and rinse the tongues in cold water. Peel the skin away from the tongues as soon as you can handle them because it is difficult to remove the skin after the tongues are cold.

Slice the peeled tongues in thick slices. Arrange the slices on a small platter, sprinkle them with salt and pepper, and garnish them with the parsley and scallions.

YERIGAMOONK / Lamb kidneys

4 servings

1 pound lamb kidneys
3 tablespoons butter
salt and pepper to taste

½ cup chopped parsley
½ cup chopped scallions

Wash the kidneys and cut them in half lengthwise. Cut out the white centers and discard them.

Melt the butter in a skillet, add the kidneys, season them with salt and pepper, and sauté them, stirring occasionally. Remove the skillet from the flame when the kidneys are well browned. Arrange the kidneys on a platter, garnish them with the parsley and scallions, and serve them immediately.

FASSOULIA PIAZ / Bean salad

6 servings

½ pound Great Northern
    beans
salt and pepper to taste
2 large tomatoes, cut into
    small wedges

1 cup chopped parsley
1 cup chopped scallions
vinegar and oil to taste

Wash the beans and place them in a saucepan with enough water to cover the beans. Cook them for 15 minutes and drain. Refill the saucepan with fresh water and add salt to taste. Simmer the beans until they are tender. Drain the beans and chill them. When the beans are cold mix in the remaining ingredients.

VARIATION: Vospov Piaz (*Lentil salad*)

Prepare this dish exactly like the one above, substituting lentils for the Great Northern beans.

FASSOULIA PLAKI / *Cold bean stew*

6 servings

½ *pound dry beans* (*Great Northern*)	*1 clove garlic, very finely chopped*
3½ *cups water* (*twice*)	⅛ *cup parsley, chopped*
½ *cup diced carrots*	*1 sprig dill, chopped*
½ *cup chopped celery*	¼ *cup tomato sauce*
1 small potato, diced	*salt and pepper to taste*
1 small onion, chopped	⅜ *cup olive oil*

Wash the beans and cook them in a saucepan with the first 3½ cups of water for 15 minutes. Drain the beans and add the second 3½ cups of water seasoned with salt. Cook the beans for 1¼ hours longer. Add the carrots, celery, potato, onion, parsley, dill, tomato sauce, and salt and pepper. Simmer the mixture for ½ hour then add the olive oil and simmer for another 15 minutes. This is delicious served cold.

VOSPOV KHEYMA / *Lentil patties*

6 servings

2 *large onions, chopped*
¼ *pound butter*
2 *cups yellow lentils*
5 *cups water*

¾ *cup fine bulghour*
1 *cup chopped parsley*
½ *cup chopped scallions*
salt to taste

Sauté the onions in butter in a skillet until they are golden brown. Set them aside. Put the lentils in a saucepan with salted water and simmer them until they are cooked (about 15 minutes). Add the browned onions with the butter from the skillet. Add the bulghour and 1 tablespoon of the parsley and stir. Cover the saucepan and simmer over a low flame for 2 minutes. Cool the mixture and shape it into patties. Arrange the patties on a platter, garnish them with the scallions and the remainder of the parsley. Serve them at once.

HUMMOS / *Chick-pea dip*

about 10 servings

1 *can chick peas (17-*
ounce can)
1 *clove garlic*
1½ *teaspoons salt*
¾ *cup lemon juice*

1 *cup taheen*
olive oil
paprika
chopped parsley

Pour the contents of the can of chick peas with its liquid into a blender. Turn the blender on until the chick peas are mashed. Add the garlic, salt, and lemon juice and blend again. Finally add the taheen and turn the blender on again for a couple of seconds.

Turn out the hummos into a wide shallow bowl. Sprinkle the top of the hummos lightiy with olive oil, paprika, and chopped parsley. Serve with lavash for dipping.

KIMIONOV KUFTA / *Sautéed cumin-flavored meat balls*

about 35 meat balls

1 pound ground lamb	1 tablespoon salt
⅓ cup bread crumbs	½ tablespoon cumin
½ cup milk	3 tablespoons butter

Combine the lamb, bread crumbs, milk, salt, and cumin in a bowl and mix thoroughly by hand. Knead the mixture like dough for 2 or 3 minutes. Form the meat into small balls about 1¼ inches in diameter. Sauté the meat balls in the butter until they are well browned on all sides. Serve hot.

The meat balls can be prepared in advance, frozen, and re-heated before serving.

YALANCHI DOLMA / *Grape leaves stuffed with an exotic rice mixture*

about 50

FILLING

3 pounds onions, chopped	½ teaspoon cinnamon
1 cup olive oil	¼ teaspoon black pepper
1 cup uncooked rice	¼ teaspoon paprika
½ cup currants	1 tablespoon salt
½ cup pine nuts	½ cup tomato sauce
½ teaspoon allspice	

Sauté the onions in olive oil in a large skillet, stirring them constantly until the onions are transparent. Add the rice, currants, pine nuts, and seasonings. Mix them well and cook the mixture for about 10 minutes longer. Add the tomato sauce. Cook the filling for another 3 minutes and set it aside to cool.

1 quart jar grape leaves   *1 cup water*
juice of ½ lemon

Wash the grape leaves in cold water to remove the brine. Take a grape leaf, remove the stem, and place it on the table with the smooth side of the leaf facing down. Place a heaping teaspoonful of the stuffing (use a little more for the larger leaves) on the stem end of the leaf. Fold the two sides of the leaf over the filling and roll the leaf from the stem end to the tip. This will resemble a short cigar after it is rolled. Continue filling and rolling the leaves and place them close together in a large saucepan. Squeeze the lemon juice into the saucepan and pour in the water. Cover the dolmas with a small plate to keep them tight. Cook over a medium flame until the liquid comes to a boil, then lower the flame as much as possible, place a cover on the pot and simmer for 1 hour. Chill the dolmas before removing them from the saucepan. Garnish the dolmas with lemon wedges and serve them cold.

MIDIA DOLMA / *Stuffed mussels*

3 dozen

3 *pounds onions, finely chopped*
1 *cup olive oil*
1 *cup uncooked rice*
½ *cup currants*
½ *cup pine nuts*
½ *teaspoon allspice*
½ *teaspoon cinnamon*
¼ *teaspoon black pepper*

¼ *teaspoon paprika*
1 *tablespoon salt*
½ *cup tomato sauce*
juice of ½ lemon
1 *cup water*
3 *dozen large mussels, with shells*
lemon wedges

Sauté the onions in the olive oil in a large skillet, stirring them constantly until the onions are transparent. Add the rice, currants, pine nuts, and seasonings. Mix them well and cook for about 10 minutes longer. Add the tomato sauce and cook for another 3 minutes. Set the filling aside to cool.

Scrub the mussel shells with a steel pad and cold water to remove all the dirt and barnacles. Remove the beards with a knife and wash them under cold running water. Drop the scrubbed mussels in a pot of cold water. With a sharp knife, force the mussel shells open (without completely detaching the shells), cut away the black waste matter attached to the flesh, and wash the inside of the shell carefully with cold water to be sure all of the sand has been washed away. Stuff each shell with a heaping tablespoonful of the filling and close the shell. Arrange the filled mussels one next to another in a large saucepan. Squeeze the lemon juice into the saucepan and pour in the water. Cover the mussels with a small plate to keep them from moving. Cook the mussels over a medium flame until the liquid comes to a boil, then lower the flame as much as possible, place a cover on the saucepan, and simmer the mussels slowly for 1 hour. Chill the mussels before removing them from the saucepan. Garnish the mussels with lemon wedges and serve cold.

TARAMA / *An appetizing dip made with carp roe*

about 8 servings

juice of 1 large lemon
⅓ cup olive oil

½ cup tarama (carp roe)
⅓ loaf of white bread

Combine the lemon juice, olive oil, and tarama in a blender. Blend the mixture until it is smooth.

Remove the crust of the bread and discard it. Wet the bread with water and then squeeze the water out of it. Add the bread to the tarama in the blender a little at a time, and blend until the mixture is smooth. Serve with lavash.

IMAM BAYELDI / *Baked eggplant*

4 to 6 servings

1 large eggplant
salt
½ cup olive oil
3 large onions, sliced
1 green pepper, chopped
2 cloves garlic, finely
     chopped

salt
⅛ teaspoon black pepper
½ cup parsley, chopped
1 tomato, chopped
½ cup tomato sauce
½ cup water

Wash and cut off the stem end of the eggplant. Cut lengthwise into quarters, and cut each piece in half across the width. Make a deep slit down the center of each piece. Sprinkle the eggplant generously with salt and set aside for ½ hour. The salt will release a dark liquid. Wash the eggplant with cold water to remove the salt and wash away the dark liquid, and dry the pieces with paper towels. Put a little olive oil in a skillet, and brown the eggplant quickly and lightly. Arrange the browned eggplant in a shallow baking dish. Combine the balance of the olive oil, onions, green pepper, garlic, 1 teaspoon salt, and pepper in the skillet. Sauté the mixture as you stir, until the onions are transparent. Add the parsley and tomato, and cook 1 minute longer. Take a tablespoon of the onion mixture and stuff it into the slit in the eggplant. Stuff the balance of the eggplant. Combine the tomato sauce and water, and add a little salt and pepper to taste. Pour this liquid into the baking dish. Bake in a 375° F. oven for 1 hour. Serve cold.

ENGUINAR / *Artichokes stuffed with white onions*

6 servings

12 white onions	1 teaspoon sugar
6 artichokes	2 tablespoons chopped dill
2 lemons	1½ cups water
2 teaspoons salt	juice of ½ lemon
¼ teaspoon black pepper	½ cup olive oil

Peel the onions and set them aside. Pull the outer layer of petals off each of the artichokes. Cut the tops of the leaves off by cutting across the artichoke halfway up and discarding the tops. Scoop out the thistlelike center of the artichoke with a teaspoon and discard it. Cut away all but 1 inch of the stem. Trim around the bottom part of the artichoke and the outer part of the stem. Rub the artichokes generously with the 2 lemons as you clean them to prevent them from turning color. Drop the artichokes and the lemons into salted water until you are ready to cook them.

Cut the cleaned artichokes in half and arrange them in a shallow saucepan. Place a cleaned white onion in the center of each artichoke half. Sprinkle them with the salt, pepper, sugar, and dill. Place a saucer upside down over the artichokes. Add the water, lemon juice, and half of the olive oil. Simmer the artichokes over a moderate flame for 35 minutes. Add the rest of the olive oil and cook them for another 10 minutes.

Chill them and serve them as a first course.

TOPIK / *A chick-pea appetizer usually made during Lent, with an exotic filling*

6 servings

FILLING

1 pound onions
¼ cup pine nuts
¼ cup currants
¾ teaspoon salt
1/16 teaspoon cayenne
⅛ teaspoon allspice
1/16 teaspoon cinnamon
½ teaspoon cumin
¼ cup taheen

Peel the onions, cut them in half and then into thin slices. Put the sliced onions in a saucepan with water to cover, and cook them until tender. Pour the cooked onions into a colander. Set aside until the water is completely drained. Combine the drained onions in a mixing bowl with the pine nuts, currants, salt, cayenne, allspice, cinnamon, cumin, and the taheen. Stir the mixture well to blend all of the flavors.

OUTER SHELL FOR THE TOPIK

½ pound chick peas   1½ teaspoon salt
1 small potato, boiled

Wash the chick peas in a bowl, cover them with warm water, and
soak overnight. The next day, drain, and remove the skins of the
chick peas. This can be done simply by crushing them with a rolling pin. Grind the chick peas in a meat grinder three times, and
then grind the boiled and peeled potato in a bowl. Add the salt,
and knead the mixture thoroughly. Moisten your hands occasionally with cold water as you knead.

Take three clean men's handkerchiefs, wet them with cold
water, and wring them dry. Place the handkerchiefs on the table.
Divide the chick-pea mixture into three portions. Place each portion in the center of each handkerchief. Roll each one with a
rolling pin to about ¼-inch thickness. Place 2 heaping tablespoonfuls of the filling in the center. Lift the four corners of the
handkerchief gently, and fold it over the filling, making sure the
filling is covered with the shell. Tie the two opposite ends of the
handkerchief, as tightly as possible, then tie the other two ends
together.

Fill a large pot with 4 quarts of water and add 4 tablespoons
of salt. Bring the water to a boil, and add the bundles of topik to
the water. Cook for 1¼ hours. Remove the topik and set aside to
cool. Remove the handkerchiefs when the topik is cold. Cut into
wedges before serving. Serve cold.

DABGADZ PATLIJAN / *Fried eggplant*

8 servings

1 large eggplant
salt
½ cup olive oil

1 clove garlic, sliced
2 tablespoons vinegar

Wash the eggplant, cut away the stem end, and peel. Cut it in half lengthwise and slice each half into ⅜-inch pieces. Sprinkle the eggplant generously with salt and set it aside for ½ hour to remove the bitter juices.

Wash the eggplant to remove the salt and dry the pieces with paper towels.

Heat the oil in a skillet. Fry the pieces of eggplant in the oil until they are golden brown. Arrange the fried eggplant in a shallow bowl alternately with the garlic. Add the vinegar and ⅛ teaspoon salt. Chill and serve.

KHOROVADZ BIBERR / *Roasted green peppers*

8 servings

6 large green peppers
1 clove garlic, sliced
⅛ teaspoon salt

3 tablespoons olive oil
1 tablespoon vinegar

Wash and dry the green peppers. Broil them over a charcoal fire or in your broiler until the skins are lightly charred.

Peel the skins, remove the stem end and discard it with the seeds. Cut the peppers into quarters lengthwise and arrange them in a shallow bowl alternately with the sliced garlic. Sprinkle with salt, add the vinegar and oil, and serve cold.

ADJEH / *A delicious parsley omelet usually made at Eastertime*
18 small omelets

4 cups parsley, or a large bunch, finely chopped	4 eggs
	1½ teaspoons salt
4 cups scallions, or 2 large bunches, finely chopped	⅛ teaspoon black pepper
	1 clove garlic, crushed
	1 cup olive oil

Combine all the ingredients except the oil in a bowl, and mix thoroughly.

Heat the olive oil in a skillet. Drop the mixture by heaping tablespoonfuls into the hot oil. Do not overcrowd the skillet. When the omelets have browned on one side, turn them over to brown the other side, and remove them to a serving platter. Continue frying the balance of the mixture. Serve cold.

JAJUKH / *Cucumber-and-yoghurt dish, refreshing for a hot summer day*

4 to 6 servings

4 cucumbers	¼ teaspoon salt
1 quart madzoon	1 clove crushed garlic
½ cup water	1 tablespoon dry mint

Wash the cucumbers and peel them. Cut the cucumbers into quarters, lengthwise, and slice them crosswise ¼ inch thick. Stir the madzoon in a bowl until it is smooth. Add the water and blend together. Add the cucumbers, salt, garlic, and dry mint, and stir. Serve cold.

abour (SOUPS)

TAN ABOUR / *Soup made with yoghurt and gorgod*

4 to 6 servings

3 *ounces gorgod*

6 *cups water*

2 *teaspoons salt*

1 *medium-sized onion,*
   finely chopped

4 *tablespoons butter*

1 *tablespoon dry mint*

1 *cup madzoon*

1 *egg*

Rinse the gorgod with cold water, and combine it with 6 cups of water in a saucepan. Bring the water to a boil and lower the flame. Add the salt to the liquid and let it simmer for 1½ hours. While the gorgod is cooking, sauté the onion in butter in a skillet until it is golden brown. Remove the skillet from the stove, add the dry mint to the onions and mix them. Pour the contents of the skillet into the saucepan when the gorgod is tender. Beat the madzoon with a spoon until it is smooth. Add the beaten egg to the madzoon, and blend thoroughly. Gradually add a little of the hot liquid from the saucepan into the madzoon mixture, stirring continuously to prevent the egg from curdling. When you have added about 2 cups of liquid into the madzoon, pour the whole mixture back into the saucepan as you stir. Continue stirring for a few minutes and remove from the fire. This soup is delicious served hot or cold.

DUTMAJ ABOUR / *Soup made with yoghurt and noodles*

4 to 6 servings

6 *tablespoons butter*
1 *large onion, chopped*
2 *quarts water*
salt to taste
2 *cups of ¼-inch-wide*
  egg noodles

1 *beaten egg*
1½ *cups madzoon*
1½ *tablespoons dry mint*

Melt the butter in a skillet and sauté the onion until it is golden brown. Boil the water in a saucepan, season with salt to taste, and add the noodles. Simmer until the noodles are tender. Stir the madzoon in a bowl until it is smooth. Add the beaten egg to the madzoon and blend well. Gradually add some of the hot water from the saucepan into the madzoon mixture, stirring continuously to prevent the egg from curdling. Now pour the madzoon mixture slowly into the saucepan as you stir. Add the mint and the contents of the skillet into the saucepan. Stir a minute longer. Serve hot.

HAV ABOUR / *Chicken soup with lemon and eggs*

4 to 6 servings

8 *cups chicken broth*
salt and pepper to taste
½ *cup orzo*

2 *beaten eggs*
juice of ½ lemon

This soup is delicious when made with a homemade chicken broth, but canned broth may be substituted. Bring the broth to a boil in a saucepan, season to taste, and add the orzo. Simmer gently until the orzo is tender. Beat the eggs vigorously in a bowl, adding the lemon juice while beating. Add very little of the hot broth to the eggs and lemon juice, mixing constantly so the eggs will not curdle. Very gradually add as much of the broth to the egg mixture as you can get in the bowl, stirring continuously. Then combine the mixture gradually with the broth in the saucepan, stirring as you pour. Continue stirring for a few minutes more and serve.

GELORIG / *An easy meat-ball stew for a cold winter night*

4 servings

1 pound chopped lamb	*4½ cups water*
2 tablespoons raw rice	*½ cup tomato sauce*
2 tablespoons parsley, finely chopped	*1 onion, sliced*
	½ cup raw rice
4 teaspoons salt	*3 carrots, scraped and cut*
¼ teaspoon black pepper	*into thick slices*

Combine the chopped lamb with the 2 tablespoons of rice, the parsley, 1 teaspoon of salt, and the pepper in a mixing bowl. Mix the ingredients by hand, and shape into meat balls about the size of a walnut. There will be about 20 meat balls.

Pour the water into a saucepan, and bring it to a boil. Add the remaining salt, the tomato sauce, sliced onion, rice, carrots and the meat balls. Bring the mixture to a boil again and lower the flame. Cover the saucepan and let it simmer for about 35 minutes.

ERISHTAH ABOUR / *Noodle soup made with lamb broth*

6 to 8 servings

6 *tablespoons butter*	*salt and pepper to taste*
1 *large onion, finely chopped*	2 *cups of ¼-inch-wide egg noodles*
2 *quarts lamb broth*	1½ *tablespoons dry mint*
½ *cup tomato sauce*	

Melt the butter in a skillet and sauté the onion until it is golden brown. Combine the broth and tomato sauce in a saucepan, and season to taste. Bring the broth to a boil, and add the noodles. Simmer until the noodles are tender. Pour the contents of the skillet into the saucepan, add the mint, and stir well. Serve hot.

TSOUG, HAV YEV MEESEGHEN

(FISH, FOWL AND MEAT)

TSOUGOV PLAKI / *Baked red snapper*

½ cup carrots, diced
1 large potato, diced
½ cup celery, diced
1 clove garlic, finely
   chopped
salt
⅛ teaspoon black pepper

1 cup water
½ cup parsley, finely
   chopped
⅓ cup tomato sauce
⅓ cup olive oil
3 pounds red snapper
1 lemon, thinly sliced

Combine the carrots, potato, celery, garlic, 1 teaspoon salt, and the black pepper with the water in a saucepan. Parboil the vegetables for about 5 to 10 minutes. Add the parsley, tomato sauce, and olive oil, and set the saucepan aside.

Wash and scrape the fish thoroughly with a knife, to be sure all of the scales have been removed. Place the fish on a baking dish and sprinkle the top lightly with salt. Pour the contents of the saucepan around the fish, and arrange the sliced lemon across the top. Bake the red snapper in a 400° F. oven for 1 hour. Baste the fish from time to time with the liquid in the pan. Serve it hot as a main dish or cold as a first course.

POROV TSOUG / *Baked stuffed striped bass*

4 to 6 servings

1 pound onions, sliced
   lengthwise
6 tablespoons olive oil
½ cup currants
½ cup pine nuts
¼ teaspoon cinnamon
¼ teaspoon allspice
1½ teaspoons salt
¼ teaspoon pepper
4 tablespoons chopped
   parsley
2 tablespoons lemon juice
3 pounds striped bass
½ cup tomato sauce
¼ cup dry white wine
1 lemon, thinly sliced

Sauté the onions in a skillet with the olive oil until the onions are transparent, without browning. Add the currants, pine nuts and seasonings, and continue cooking as you stir the mixture for a few minutes.

Add the parsley and lemon juice, and stir the mixture. Have the fish slit through the side, and the backbone removed, but be sure the other side of the fish remains attached. Wash the fish thoroughly, and scrape the skin with a knife to make sure all the scales have been removed. Place the fish in a baking dish. Lift the top half of the fish, and fill the center with the onion mixture. Spread the stuffing evenly on the fish and cover with the top half. Dilute the tomato sauce with the wine and pour this over the fish. Arrange the sliced lemon over the fish. Bake in a 375° F. oven for 45 minutes, or until the fish flakes when tested with a fork. Serve cold.

AJEM PILAF / *Persian pilaf with chicken*

5 to 6 servings

3 cups chicken broth
salt and pepper to taste
2½ cups raw rice
¼ teaspoon allspice

5 pounds chicken, cut into
serving pieces
3 tablespoons butter

Heat the chicken broth in a saucepan, and season it with salt and pepper to taste. When the broth comes to a boil, add the rice and allspice. Let the broth come to a boil again, lower the flame, and cover the saucepan. Let the rice simmer slowly, until the liquid is absorbed.

Wash the chicken thoroughly, and arrange the pieces in a casserole. Sprinkle salt and pepper over the chicken, and add the partially cooked rice over the chicken. Dot with butter and place a cover on the casserole. The steam from the hot rice will be enough to complete the cooking of the rice and the chicken without any additional liquid. Bake in a 375° F. oven for 2 to 2½ hours.

POROV HAV / *Roast stuffed chicken*

4 to 5 servings

FILLING

1 small onion, finely
chopped
2 tablespoons butter
1 cup raw rice
¼ cup pine nuts

¼ teaspoon allspice
1 teaspoon salt
⅛ teaspoon black pepper
¼ cup currants
1 cup chicken broth

Combine the onion and butter in a saucepan and sauté the onion until it is transparent. Add the rice and pine nuts, and sauté the mixture a minute longer as you stir. Add the allspice, salt and pepper, currants, and the broth. Bring the mixture to a boil and lower the flame as much as possible. Cover the saucepan and simmer until the liquid is absorbed.

CHICKEN

4–5-pound roasting
    chicken or capon

Singe the chicken over a flame and wash it thoroughly. Sprinkle lightly with salt and pepper, inside and out. Fill the chicken with the rice mixture, and sew the opening with a large needle and thread. Place the stuffed chicken in a roasting pan, and add 2 cups of water to the pan. Place the pan into a 375° F. oven and bake for 2 hours.

SHISH KEBAB / Marinated lamb on skewers

6 servings

1 leg of lamb	1/4 teaspoon pepper
2 large onions, thinly sliced	1/8 cup olive oil
1 1/2 teaspoons oregano	1/4 cup dry red wine
2 teaspoons freshly ground coriander	2 pounds white onions
1 tablespoon salt	6 green peppers
	6 tomatoes (optional)

Ask your butcher to bone and cut a leg of lamb into 2-inch cubes for shish kebab. Have him remove most of the fat and all of the gristle. Marinate the meat in a large bowl with the sliced onions, seasonings, oil, and wine. Mix the ingredients well to be sure that all of the pieces of meat are equally coated. Cover the bowl and let it marinate in the refrigerator overnight.

Peel the white onions, put them on skewers and broil over a charcoal fire until they are brown. Broil the whole green peppers and some small tomatoes if you like. Always broil the vegetables before the meat and keep them warm in a covered casserole until the lamb is ready. Place the meat on skewers being careful to spear each piece through the center. Broil the lamb, turning from time to time until the meat is browned. Be sure not to overcook the meat. Shish kebab tastes best when it is juicy. Add the sliced onions to the cooked meat. Serve the meat and vegetables with bulghour pilaf.

TASS KEBAB / *Potted lamb*

6 servings

3 *pounds boned leg of lamb*
4 *tablespoons butter*
2 *chopped onions*

½ *cup tomato sauce*
salt and pepper to taste
2 *cups water*

Cut the lamb into 1½-inch squares. Melt the butter in a large skillet and sauté the meat in the butter until it browns. Remove the lamb to a covered pot. Sauté the onions in the same skillet and then combine them with the meat. Add the tomato sauce, seasonings, and water. Cover the pot and cook over a low flame for 1½ hours, stirring occasionally until the meat is tender and most of the liquid has evaporated.

Make a well in a serving of pilaf, fill it with some tass kebab and its gravy.

KHEYMA KEBAB / *Chopped lamburgers broiled on skewers*

8 to 10 servings

3 *medium onions, very finely chopped*
2 *tablespoons salt*
1 *tablespoon paprika*
1½ *cups parsley, very finely chopped*

5 *pounds boned leg of lamb, ground twice with a very fine blade*

Combine the onions with the salt in a mixing bowl. Crush and squeeze the mixture with your hand, add the paprika and parsley, and mix. Add the chopped lamb to the bowl and knead the mixture for 5 to 10 minutes.

Take a portion (about the size of a small orange) of the meat mixture in your hand, roll it into a ball, and push a skewer through the center of it. Squeeze the meat on the skewer into the shape of a frankfurter or long sausage around the skewer. Add as many kebabs to the skewer as the length of it will comfortably hold. Continue putting the rest of the meat on skewers. Broil the kebabs quickly over a charcoal fire and serve hot with the garnish below.

Serve with pilaf.

GARNISH

1½ *cups chopped parsley*
3 *medium onions, thinly sliced*

1 *teaspoon paprika*

Mix the ingredients and serve with the Kheyma Kebab.

LULE KEBAB / *Baked lamburgers*

6 servings

2½ pounds chopped lamb
½ cup bread crumbs
2 teaspoons salt
½ teaspoon black pepper
1 tablespoon ground
    coriander

2 ounces milk
1 bunch parsley, finely
    chopped
1 bunch scallions, finely
    chopped

Combine the chopped lamb, bread crumbs, salt and pepper, coriander, and milk in a mixing bowl. Mix the ingredients with your hand and knead until they are well blended. Form the mixture into sausage shapes and arrange them in a baking dish. Bake in a 375° F. oven for 1 hour. Turn kebabs once to be sure both sides are browned. Place in a serving dish and sprinkle with the chopped parsley and scallions. Serve hot.

KUFTA / *Armenian meat balls with an exotic filling*

6 servings

FILLING

1 pound shoulder of lamb,
    chopped (with some of
    the fat left on the
    meat)
3 large onions, finely
    chopped
salt and pepper to taste

⅛ teaspoon allspice
⅛ teaspoon cinnamon
1 tablespoon freshly ground
    coriander
½ cup chopped walnuts or
    pine nuts

Sauté the meat in a skillet over a moderate flame, stirring occasionally. When the meat is partially cooked, push it to one side in the pan, and add the onions to the other side of the pan. Sauté the onions until they are transparent. Add the seasonings and mix all of the ingredients in the skillet. Continue cooking the mixture for 20 to 30 minutes, stirring frequently, until the meat is cooked and begins to brown slightly. Remove from flame. Add the nuts and cool. It is best to prepare the filling a day ahead to allow the mixture to be chilled.

KHEYMA

¾ cup very fine bulghour
½ cup cold water
1 pound very lean lamb, cut from a leg of lamb, ground twice (reserve bones)

salt and pepper to taste
1 tablespoon freshly ground coriander
8 cups broth
½ cup tomato sauce (optional)

Mix the bulghour and the water in a mixing bowl. Add the meat, salt, pepper, and coriander to the bulghour and knead like dough. Moisten your hands with cold water occasionally as you knead the mixture. Continue kneading for 15 to 20 minutes. Wet your hands again and from a bit of the mixture make a ball about the size of a large walnut. Hold the ball in your hand and form it into a cone shape. Press the index finger of your other hand into the center and press it all around the inside wall, to make a round opening. The wall should be as thin as possible without breaking. Place a spoonful of the filling in the opening and then seal it gently and securely by pushing the opening together until it is closed and smoothing the surface with wet fingers. Flatten it slightly by pressing gently with the palm of your hand to give the kufta a base. Continue making the kuftas until you finish the mixture. It should make approximately 16 kuftas.

Cook some lamb bones in salted water for about 1½ hours. Remove the scum, strain the broth, and add 6 tablespoons of tomato sauce if desired.

Drop the kuftas one at a time into the boiling broth and cook uncovered for about 10 minutes or until the kuftas rise to the top of the pot. Serve with or without the broth.

Kufta is good served with madzoon and a mixed salad.

MADZOONABOUROV KUFTA / *Kufta served with a madzoon soup*

8 servings

1 recipe of kufta (page 35)	*1 tablespoon salt*
	1 egg
3 pounds lamb bones with meat on them	*3 cups madzoon*
	2 tablespoons dry mint

Put the lamb into a large saucepan with enough water to cover and add the salt. Bring the liquid to a boil and lower the flame. Remove the scum from the surface as it forms. Simmer for 1½–2 hours, adding water as it evaporates. You should have 2 quarts of broth by the time the meat is tender. Pour the broth through a strainer into another large saucepan, chill it overnight, and remove the fat from the surface the next day.

When the meat is cool enough to handle, remove it from the bones, discard the bones, and set the meat aside. Follow the recipe and the directions for kufta on page 35. Make each kufta no larger than a walnut, and roll it in your hands into a round ball. Continue making the balance of the kuftas.

Bring the broth to a boil, and drop the kuftas into it. Cook the kuftas for 5 minutes. Beat the egg and madzoon in a bowl until they are well blended and smooth. Gradually add 2 cups of the hot broth to the madzoon mixture, stirring continuously. Pour the madzoon mixture gradually into the saucepan, as you stir. Add the dry mint and the boiled lamb into the saucepan. Heat over a very low flame as you stir, and serve in soup bowls.

CHI KUFTA / *Steak tartare . . . Armenian style*

6 servings

¾ cup very fine bulghour
½ cup cold water
1 pound very lean leg of lamb, ground twice
salt and pepper to taste
1 pinch cayenne

1 medium onion, finely chopped
1 cup parsley, finely chopped
1 bunch scallions, very finely sliced

Combine the bulghour and water in a mixing bowl and mix them until the bulghour soaks in the water. Add the meat and seasonings and knead the mixture like dough. Moisten your hands with cold water occasionally as you knead the mixture. Add the chopped onion and a heaping tablespoon of parsley and continue to knead the mixture. After kneading for a total of 10 minutes, taste a bit of the kufta to be sure the bulghour is no longer crunchy.

Shape the kufta into small patties and arrange them on a platter. Garnish the chi kufta with the rest of the parsley and the scallions and serve it at once.

This is especially good with tomatesov salata and a tall glass of tan.

SINI KUFTA / *Baked kufta*

6 servings

1 *recipe of kufta and*   ½ *cup water*
filling (page 35)
4 *tablespoons butter,*
softened

Prepare the kufta and filling as on page 35.

Divide the kufta into two portions. Spread one portion evenly into a buttered 9 × 9-inch baking dish. Wet your hand with cold water to smooth the layer. Spread the filling over the first layer evenly. Wet your hands with cold water again, and take a small amount of the balance of the kufta. Flatten it out in the palm of your hands, and place it over the filling. Continue with the balance of the kufta until you have covered the surface of the filling. Smooth the surface with your hand, and spread the soft butter over it. Cut through with a knife into diamond-shaped pieces about 2 × 3 inches.

Sprinkle the surface with the water, and bake in a 400° F. oven for 45 minutes.

DABGADZ KUFTA / *Pan-browned meat balls*

6 servings

1 *recipe of kufta and*   ⅓ *cup water*
filling (page 35)
4 *tablespoons melted*
butter

Prepare the kuftas with the filling as on page 35. These kuftas should be made the size and shape of an egg. Place the kuftas in a baking dish with the melted butter. Shake the pan to coat the kuftas with the melted butter. Sprinkle the water over the kuftas, and bake in a 375° F. oven for 35 to 45 minutes. Shake the pan from time to time until the kuftas are lightly browned on all sides.

BAKI KUFTA / *Kufta served as a main dish during Lent in place of meat or as a meza any time*

6 to 8 servings
(as the main course)

STUFFING FOR KUFTA

1 pound chopped onions (4 cups)	*2 teaspoons salt*
⅓ cup olive oil	*½ cup pine nuts*
½ teaspoon allspice	*½ cup currants*
½ teaspoon cumin	*¼ cup chopped parsley*
⅛ teaspoon cayenne	*⅔ cup taheen*

Sauté the onions in a skillet with the olive oil. Stir them continuously until they are tender but not brown. Add the seasonings, pine nuts, currants, and parsley and stir until they are well blended. Remove the skillet from the stove, add the taheen, and stir the mixture again. The stuffing should be well chilled before use so it is best to prepare it a day in advance.

VARIATION STUFFING

1½ pounds chopped onions (6 cups)	¼ cup chopped parsley
½ cup olive oil	½ cup cooked chick peas
¼ teaspoon black pepper	1 cup coarsely chopped walnuts
2½ teaspoons salt	

Combine the onions and olive oil in a skillet. Sauté the onions until they are tender without browning them, stirring continuously. Add the rest of the ingredients as you stir, and cook them for a few minutes longer. The stuffing should be well chilled before use.

SHELL FOR KUFTA

1½ cups fine bulghour	1 teaspoon cumin
½ cup water	½ teaspoon paprika
1 cup cooked chick peas	5 teaspoons salt
1 cup farina	2 tablespoons lemon juice

Place the bulghour in a mixing bowl, add the water, and set the bowl aside for 5 minutes.

Remove and discard the skins of the chick peas and grind them with the fine blade of a meat grinder. Add the chick peas, farina, cumin, paprika, and 3 teaspoons salt to the bulghour in the bowl. Knead the mixture. Wet your hands from time to time as you knead the mixture. As you knead you will see that the mixture will hold together and feel firmer. Continue kneading for 12 to 15 minutes.

With a bit of the mixture (about the size of a golf ball) make a ball, then form it into a cone shape. Press your index finger into the base of the cone, and press it all around the inside wall to make an opening without breaking it. The wall should be about ¼ inch thick. Place a spoonful of the filling into the opening and seal it gently and securely by pushing the opening together until it is closed. Be sure the filling does not ooze out. Smooth the surface of the kufta gently and roll it into a round ball. Continue making the kuftas until you have used all of the stuffing and shell mixture. This should make approximately 24 kuftas.

Boil 1½ quarts of water in a kettle, and add 2 teaspoons of salt and the lemon juice. Gently drop about 6 or 8 kuftas into the boiling water at a time. Bring the water to a boil again and simmer the kuftas for 10 minutes or until they rise to the surface. Remove the kuftas gently and continue cooking the balance. Chill and serve.

IZMIR KUFTA / *Hamburgers, Smyrna style*

4 servings

1 pound chopped lamb
1 medium onion, finely chopped
2 tablespoons parsley, finely chopped
2 slices white bread, soaked in water and squeezed dry
1 teaspoon salt
⅛ teaspoon black pepper
2 tablespoons butter

Combine the meat, onion, parsley, bread, salt, and pepper in a mixing bowl. Mix the ingredients by hand, and knead the mixture as for dough. Shape the mixture into patties. Melt the butter in a skillet and brown the patties on both sides. This will take a few minutes on each side. Serve immediately.

LAHMAJOON / *Armenian meat pies*

about 12 servings

DOUGH

⅓ cup warm water	1 tablespoon sugar
1 package yeast	1 cup warm milk
4 cups flour	¼ cup butter, melted
1 teaspoon salt	

Put ⅓ cup of warm water into a small bowl, and add the contents of a package of yeast to it. Set aside until the yeast has dissolved.

Combine the flour, salt, and sugar in a large mixing bowl. Make a well in the center of the flour mixture. The milk and butter should be warm enough for you to be able to put your hand into it without feeling too hot. Pour the milk, butter, and the yeast mixture into the center of the flour. Knead the mixture with your hands. Add a little more milk or flour if needed. Continue kneading until the dough is well blended and smooth. This should be a soft dough. Cover the bowl with a sheet of aluminum foil and a towel over it. Set the bowl in a warm place and cover it again with a blanket or coat to keep it warm. Allow the dough to rise for 2 to 3 hours.

FILLING

2 pounds chopped lamb	1 clove garlic, mashed
1 cup parsley, finely chopped	1 large can Italian tomatoes in sauce
1 green pepper, finely chopped	1 tablespoon salt
	⅛ teaspoon black pepper
1 large onion, finely chopped	1 tablespoon dry mint
	pinch of cayenne

Combine the chopped meat with all the vegetables and seasonings in a large mixing bowl. Be sure the vegetables are chopped as fine as possible, and crush the tomatoes that come out of the can. Mix the ingredients by hand to be sure they are well blended.

When the dough has raised to double its size, it is ready. Cut the dough into walnut-sized pieces. There should be about 35 pieces in total. Roll each piece into a ball with your hands, using a little flour as needed to prevent sticking. Sprinkle the table lightly with flour, and arrange the balls of dough on the flour. Cover the dough with a towel.

Sprinkle some flour on the table, place a ball of dough on the flour, sprinkle the dough again with flour and roll it out with a rolling pin to 5 or 6 inches in diameter. Arrange as many pieces of rolled dough on a cookie sheet as the pan will hold. Take about ⅓ of a cupful of the meat mixture, and spread it evenly by hand on each rolled circle. Spread the mixture out, leaving about ¼-inch margin around the edge. Preheat the oven to 450° F. Place one oven rack on the bottom of the oven, and the other as high as you can. Place the cookie sheet on the lower rack in the oven for 6 to 8 minutes, then move the cookie sheet to the upper rack for 5 minutes, until the lahmajoon browns lightly. Continue preparing and baking the balance of the pies. Lahmajoon keeps very well in a freezer, and is nice to have on hand when you are in a hurry or have unexpected guests.

To reheat frozen lahmajoons, arrange them on a cookie sheet, and place one face up and one face down on top of it to keep the filling from drying out. Heat them, turn them right side up, stack them, and serve.

KESHKEG / *Lamb and gorgod, cooked to the consistency and appearance of oatmeal*

6 servings

¾ cup gorgod

4 pounds shoulder of
   lamb, bone in, cut into
   large pieces as for stew

salt and pepper to taste

Wash the gorgod in cold water and drain it. Wash the meat in cold water, and combine it with the gorgod in a large saucepan. Add enough water to cover the meat. Place the saucepan on the stove, and bring the liquid to a boil. Lower the flame, and let it simmer. Remove any scum that forms on top of the mixture. Add salt and pepper. After 3 or 4 hours of cooking, the meat will fall off the bones. Remove the bones and any fat that may have been on the meat. Stir the mixture from time to time to prevent it from sticking to the bottom of the saucepan. At this point it is best to place an asbestos plate between the flame and the saucepan. With a large, long-handled spoon, crush the meat and gorgod mixture against the inside of the saucepan. This should be done as often as possible without tiring your arm too much. Continue cooking for several hours until the meat and the gorgod are well blended. Add water as needed when the mixture thickens.

BUTTER SAUCE

¼ pound butter

1 teaspoon paprika

cumin

Melt the butter in a small saucepan, add the paprika, and stir well.

When serving the keshkeg, make a well in the center, and pour in 1 to 2 tablespoons of the hot butter. Sprinkle lightly with cumin.

MANTI / *Meat-filled pastry boats baked and served with mad-zoon*

6 servings

1 *pound chopped lamb*	1 *egg*
1 *onion, finely chopped*	2 *tablespoons melted butter*
2 *tablespoons parsley,*	1 *cup warm water*
finely chopped	⅛ *pound melted butter*
1½ *teaspoons salt*	6 *cups chicken broth*
⅛ *teaspoon pepper*	*madzoon*
3¼ *cups flour*	

Combine the meat with the onion, parsley, 1 teaspoon salt, and pepper. Mix them thoroughly and set them aside.

Combine the flour, ½ teaspoon salt, egg, 2 tablespoons melted butter, and the warm water in a mixing bowl. Knead the dough until it is smooth. Divide the dough into two balls and cover them with a towel to keep them warm. Let them rest for ½ hour.

Take a rolling pin and roll each ball of dough to a thickness of ⅛ inch. Cut the rolled dough into 1½-inch squares and fill each square with a small amount of the meat mixture (about the size of a marble). Pinch the two ends of the dough together to resemble a boat. Continue making the boats until all of the dough has been used. Put the ⅛ pound of melted butter in a baking pan, and arrange the filled boats (manti) in the pan, one next to another. Bake in a 375° F. oven for ½ hour or until the manti is lightly browned. Add the hot chicken broth to the pan and bake for 5 minutes longer.

Serve in individual dishes with a little of the broth. Add 2 or 3 tablespoons of madzoon to the center of each serving.

SHISHBOEREG / *This hearty soup is filled with small stuffed dumplings, chick peas, and homemade croutons. It is so delicious and so hearty that my family prefers having it as a main dish. The dumplings can be made ahead and stored in the freezer. The croutons, too, can be made in advance and stored in the refrigerator.*

about 6 servings

MEAT STUFFING FOR DUMPLINGS

½ *pound chopped lamb*
½ *teaspoon salt*
2 *tablespoons onion,
     finely chopped*

2 *tablespoons parsley, finely
     chopped*

Combine the meat with the salt, onion, and parsley. Mix well and set aside until ready to use.

DOUGH FOR DUMPLINGS

2 *cups flour*
½ *teaspoon salt*
3 *eggs (extra large)*

2 *tablespoons olive oil*
1 *tablespoon milk*

Combine the flour and salt in a bowl. Make a well in the center. Add the eggs, olive oil, and milk into the well and blend with the flour. Knead the dough for 15 minutes. Wrap the dough with a sheet of aluminum foil and cover the foil with a towel to keep the dough warm. Let the dough rest for 30 minutes since this makes it easier to roll out later. Cut the dough into four pieces and roll one piece at a time with a rolling pin, keeping the balance of the dough covered. Roll the dough as thin as possible (about $\frac{1}{16}$ inch thick). Cut the rolled dough into 1¼-inch squares. Take a bit of the meat mixture (size of a large pea) and place it in the center of a square of dough. Fold half of the square of dough over the meat in a triangular shape and pinch the edges to seal. Bend the two outer corners to meet and pinch them together. Continue making the dumplings until the balance of the dough has been used. This makes about 180 dumplings.

CROUTONS

1 cup flour	*½ cup water*
4 tablespoons butter	*1 cup cooking oil*
½ teaspoon salt	

Blend the flour, butter, and salt together in a mixing bowl. Add the water to the mixture and knead the dough for a minute or two. Divide the dough into quarters. Take one piece at a time and roll it out on the table with your hands into a long rope about the thickness of your small finger. Cut the dough into ½-inch pieces with a knife. When all the dough has been prepared, heat the cooking oil in a skillet. Fry the croutons slowly until they are golden brown.

SOUP

2 *quarts chicken broth*	2 *tablespoons lemon juice*
salt and pepper to taste	2 *garlic cloves crushed and*
1 10-ounce can chick peas	*mixed with the juice of 1*
½ *tablespoon dry mint*	*lemon (optional)*

About ½ hour before you are ready to serve the soup, bring the broth to a boil in a large saucepan. Season it with salt and pepper. Drop the dumplings into the boiling broth, lower the flame, and simmer the dumplings for about 20 minutes. Test one dumpling to make sure the dough is tender but still firm. Drain the liquid from the can of chick peas. Add the chick peas to the broth and simmer for another minute or two. Remove the saucepan from the flame. Add the dry mint and the lemon juice and stir. Serve the soup at once. Garnish it with the croutons and if desired with the garlic sauce.

Shishboereg makes a fine winter meal with a healthy salad on the side.

PACHA / *A special lamb stew prepared with lamb tongues and calves' feet*

6 servings

4 *calves' feet*	*salt and pepper to taste*
2 *cloves garlic*	6 *lamb tongues*

Singe and scrape the calves' feet to be sure they are clean. Wash them thoroughly, and place them in a large kettle, with water to cover. Bring the mixture to a boil, and lower the flame to let it simmer. Remove the scum from time to time. Add the garlic, salt and pepper, and cook for about 5 hours. Trim and wash the tongues. Place them in a saucepan, with water to cover, and salt to taste. Cook the tongues until they are tender. Drain the water and remove the skin from the tongues, while they are still hot. Add the peeled tongues to the kettle and cook for 1 hour longer. Remove all the bones. Serve in soup bowls as a main course.

KHABOURGA / *Roasted stuffed lamb*

4 to 6 servings

*7- to 8-pound rack of lamb
(loin and ribs with
breast)*

FILLING

4 lamb kidneys
3 tablespoons butter
*1 small onion, finely
chopped*
1 cup raw rice
¼ cup pine nuts

¼ teaspoon allspice
1 teaspoon salt
⅛ teaspoon black pepper
¼ cup currants
1 cup broth

Wash the kidneys, cut them in half, and remove the white center. Cut the kidneys into small pieces and place them in a skillet with 1 tablespoon butter. Sauté the kidneys until they are well browned, and set them aside. Sauté the onion in 2 tablespoons of butter in a saucepan until it is transparent. Add the rice and pine nuts to the saucepan and sauté mixture another minute as you stir. Add the allspice, salt and pepper, currants, sautéed kidneys, and the broth. Bring the mixture to a boil, and lower the flame as much as possible. Cover the saucepan and simmer until the liquid is absorbed. The rice will be partially cooked.

Ask your butcher to trim as much fat as possible from the breast of lamb and to make a pocket in the breast. Sprinkle the lamb lightly with salt and pepper, inside and outside. Open the pocket and fill it with the rice filling. Sew the opening with a large needle and thread, and place the stuffed lamb in a large roasting pan, fat side up. Add 2 cups of water to the roasting pan, and bake in a 400° F. oven for 1½ hours. Baste the meat from time to time with the juices in the pan.

KHAVOURMA / *Braised lamb*

4 to 5 servings

2½ *pounds boneless lamb*	2 *teaspoons salt*
2 *cups water*	¼ *teaspoon black pepper*

Cut the lamb into 1½-inch cubes. Combine the lamb and water in a saucepan. Add the salt and pepper, cover the saucepan, and cook over a low flame for 1½ hours, stirring occasionally. When the liquid has evaporated, braise the meat in its own juices. Turn the meat continuously until the pieces are lightly browned on all sides. This will take about 5 to 10 minutes. Serve with pilaf.

JIGERR / *Lamb liver with smothered onions*

4 to 5 servings

3 *tablespoons butter*	*salt and pepper*
1 *lamb liver, cut into thick slices*	1 *large onion, sliced*

Melt the butter in a skillet. Wash and wipe the liver slices dry, and place them in the skillet. Sprinkle the liver with salt and pepper, and brown them quickly, for medium and juicy liver. Turn the slices and brown the other side. Remove the liver to a serving platter. Add the sliced onion to the same skillet. Sprinkle salt and pepper on the onion, and sauté until it is lightly browned. Cover the liver with the sautéed onion and serve immediately.

BOOMBAR / *Stuffed lamb casings*

4 to 6 servings

½ *pound lamb casings, cleaned and salted*
2 *pounds chopped shoulder of lamb*
2 *cups large bulghour*
4 *tablespoons dry mint*
salt and pepper to taste
kettle of lamb broth
butter

Wash the casings thoroughly, rubbing them well to remove all the salt. Take one casing at a time, slip one end over the faucet and let the cold water run through it. Then soak the casings in cold water for 2 hours.

Combine the chopped lamb, bulghour, mint, and seasonings and mix them well. Wet your hands occasionally and knead the mixture as you would knead dough for a few minutes.

Tie a knot at one end of a piece of casing and turn it inside out, using a dull-edged knife to push it through. When you have turned the casing, hold the knotted end in your hand and push the knot back into the casing in position to turn right side out again. Start filling the meat mixture into the opening created by pushing the knot back into the casing. As you fill it the knot will slip down leaving more of an opening to fill. Continue filling the casing until the entire casing has slipped through itself and is right side out again. Adjust the amount of meat in the casing by squeezing it gently to equalize it. Be sure you do not pack it tightly. It needs room for swelling as it cooks. Fill all of the casings in the same manner.

Season the lamb broth and bring it to a boil. Add the boombar to the kettle and cover it. Simmer the boombar for 20 minutes, then prick the casings every few inches to allow the broth to penetrate them. Let the boombar cook in the kettle for a total of 2¼ hours, adding water to the kettle as the liquid evaporates.

Arrange the boombar in a large baking pan with some dabs of butter. Bake the boombar at 450° F., turning them as needed until they are lightly browned.

MEESOV GERAGOORNERR

(MEAT WITH VEGETABLES)

The Armenians love stuffed vegetables and they stuff almost every kind from cabbage leaves to baby eggplants. They are called dolmas. A few of the varieties follow.

PATLIJANOV DOLMA / *Eggplant stuffed with a bulghour and lamb mixture*

4 to 6 servings

1 pound chopped lamb
¼ cup large bulghour
1 onion, finely chopped
salt
⅛ teaspoon pepper

½ cup tomato sauce
12 baby eggplants
1½ cups water
juice of ½ lemon

Combine the chopped lamb, bulghour, onion, 1 teaspoon salt, pepper, and half of the tomato sauce in a bowl. Mix the ingredients thoroughly with your hand. Wash the eggplants with cold water. Cut off the stem end, and with an apple corer, scoop out the pulp of the eggplant and leave only the thin purple shell. Fill the eggplants with the meat mixture, and arrange them in a saucepan. Combine the water with the balance of the tomato sauce, the lemon juice, and a little salt to taste, and pour the liquid into the saucepan. Bring the liquid to a boil, and lower the flame. Place a cover on the saucepan, and simmer for 45 minutes. Serve hot with madzoon.

DEREV DOLMA / *Grape leaves stuffed with a bulghour and lamb mixture*

4 servings

FILLING

1 pound chopped lamb	*1 teaspoon salt*
¼ cup large bulghour	*⅛ teaspoon black pepper*
1 onion, finely chopped	*½ cup tomato sauce*

Combine the chopped lamb, bulghour, onion, salt, pepper, and half of the tomato sauce in a mixing bowl. Knead the ingredients by hand until they are well blended.

1 pint jar grape leaves	*1½ cups water*
juice of ½ lemon	

Wash the grape leaves in cold water to remove the brine. Take a grape leaf, remove the stem, and place it on the table with the smooth side of the leaf face down. Place a heaping tablespoonful of the meat mixture on the stem end of the leaf. Fold the two sides of the leaf over the filling and roll the leaf from the stem end to the tip. This should resemble a short cigar after it is rolled. Continue filling and rolling the leaves and place them close together in a saucepan. Cover the dolmas with a small plate to keep them from moving. Add the lemon juice, the balance of the tomato sauce, and the water to the saucepan. Cover the saucepan, bring the liquid to a boil over a moderate flame, then lower the flame and simmer the dolmas for 45 minutes. Serve hot with madzoon.

LAHANA DOLMA / *Cabbage dolma stuffed with lamb*

4 servings

1 solid head of cabbage	*⅔ cup tomato sauce*
1 pound ground shoulder of lamb with some of the fat removed	*salt and pepper to taste*
	1½ cups water
¼ cup rice	*1 heaping tablespoon sugar*
1 medium onion, chopped	*juice of ½ lemon*

Cut around the root of the cabbage with a knife and place the cabbage in a pot of boiling salted water. Bring the water back to a boil and cook the cabbage for about 5 minutes. Drain and remove the outer leaves, taking care not to tear them. Discard the inner leaves or save them for another use.

Mix the meat, rice, onion, half of the tomato sauce, and the salt and pepper by hand. Take one leaf of cabbage at a time, cut away the center vein to leave two pieces. Place a spoonful of the meat mixture in the center of one piece of cabbage and roll it up.

Arrange the dolmas in a saucepan as you make them. Place them side by side and in layers until they are all made. Add the water, the balance of the tomato sauce, sugar, lemon juice, and salt and pepper to taste. Cover and simmer slowly for 1 hour. Serve with madzoon.

SOKHOV DOLMA / *Onions stuffed with lamb*

4 servings

10 large onions

2 pounds ground shoulder of lamb

½ cup rice

1 cup tomato sauce

salt and pepper to taste

12 prunes

juice of ½ lemon

2 cups water

Peel the onions and make a slit down one side of each. Drop the onions into boiling salted water and parboil them for 5 minutes or until the layers of the onions can be separated. Drain and cool the onions.

Combine the meat, rice, half of the tomato sauce, and the salt and pepper and mix them well. Separate all the layers of the onions and stuff each of the layers with a heaping spoonful of the meat mixture. Fold the layers around the meat into an oval shape. Place them one next to another in a saucepan scattering the prunes around them. Add the rest of the tomato sauce, the lemon juice, salt and pepper, and the 2 cups of water. Cover the saucepan and cook the dolmas over a low flame for 45 minutes.

TUTUMOV DOLMA / *Zucchini stuffed with lamb*

4 servings

8 zucchini squash

1 pound ground shoulder of lamb

½ cup tomato sauce

¼ cup rice

salt and pepper to taste

1 medium onion, finely chopped

½ teaspoon basil

1½ cups water

juice of ¼ lemon

Wash the squash thoroughly to be sure any sand has been removed from the skin. Cut each of them in half and with an apple corer scoop out as much of the inside as you can leaving about ¼ inch of zucchini shell.

Combine the meat with half of the tomato sauce, the rice, the salt and pepper, the onion, the basil. Mix them well. Take a little of the mixture at a time and fill it into the zucchini. Arrange the filled zucchinis in a saucepan. Add the water, the remainder of the tomato sauce, salt and pepper to taste, and the lemon juice. Cover the saucepan and simmer the dolma over a low flame for about 40 minutes or until the squash is tender. The dolma should be served with madzoon.

TOMATES DOLMA / *Baked stuffed tomatoes*

4 servings

3 tablespoons butter	¼ teaspoon allspice
1 pound chopped beef or lamb	3 tablespoons chopped parsley
1 medium onion, chopped	salt and pepper to taste
⅛ cup rice	8 medium tomatoes
⅛ cup pine nuts	sugar
¼ teaspoon cinnamon	melted butter

Melt the butter in a skillet, and add the meat. Stir the meat to break it up, and sauté until it is lightly browned. Add the onion and sauté until it is transparent. Add the rice, pine nuts, cinnamon, allspice, chopped parsley, and salt and pepper. Stir the mixture and cook for a few minutes longer.

Wash the tomatoes, and cut across the stem end, leaving it

attached at one side. The top will be used as a cover for the tomato. Scoop out as much of the pulp of the tomato as possible with a teaspoon and reserve it. Fill the tomatoes with the meat mixture, close the top with the cover, and arrange them, cover side down, in a baking dish. If you have a blender, put the tomato pulp into the blender to liquefy it. If not, just dice the pulp with a knife. Season the tomato pulp with salt and sugar. Pour the tomato pulp into the baking dish around the stuffed tomatoes. Brush the tops of the stuffed tomatoes with melted butter, and bake in a 375° F. oven for ½ hour. Sprinkle the top of each tomato with ½ teaspoon of sugar, and bake them for another 30 minutes. Serve hot.

MOUSSAKA / Eggplant and lamb casserole

4 to 6 servings

1 large eggplant
¼ pound butter
1 pound chopped lamb
salt and pepper to taste
1 onion, finely chopped

½ cup tomato sauce
½ cup water
½ cup parsley, finely chopped

Wash the eggplant, and cut the stem end off. Slice the eggplant crosswise into slices ⅜ inch thick. Place the slices on a plate, and sprinkle them generously with salt. This will release some of the bitter juices in the eggplant. Set aside for 1 hour.

Combine 1 tablespoon of butter with the chopped lamb in a skillet. Add salt and pepper and stir the mixture. When the meat is lightly browned, add the onion and cook until the onion is softened. Add the tomato sauce diluted with the water, and the parsley. Stir the mixture and cook a minute longer.

Wash the eggplant slices to remove the excess salt, and pat them dry with paper towels. Brown the eggplant lightly in a skillet with butter. Arrange half of the browned eggplant in a 7 × 11-inch baking dish. Spread the meat mixture over the layer of eggplant. Arrange the balance of the eggplant over the meat. Bake in a 375° F. oven for 45 minutes. Serve with pilaf.

PATLIJAN KARNI YAREK / *Baked stuffed eggplant*

4 servings

1 large eggplant	*¼ cup pine nuts*
4 tablespoons butter	*½ cup parsley, finely*
1 pound chopped lamb	*chopped*
salt and pepper to taste	*¼ teaspoon allspice*
1 large onion, finely	*1 cup tomato sauce*
chopped	*1 large tomato, sliced*
1 green pepper, finely	*½ cup water*
chopped	

Wash the eggplant, and cut the stem end off. Cut the eggplant lengthwise into quarters, and place the pieces on a plate. Sprinkle the eggplant generously with salt, and set it aside for 1 hour.

Combine 1 tablespoon of butter with the chopped lamb in a skillet. Add salt and pepper, and stir the mixture.

When the meat is lightly browned, add the onion and sauté the mixture until the onion is softened. Add the green pepper, pine nuts, parsley, allspice, and ½ cup of the tomato sauce. Stir the mixture and simmer for 5 minutes.

Wash the eggplant to remove the excess salt, and pat it dry with paper towels. Brown the eggplant lightly with the balance of the butter in a skillet. Arrange the browned eggplant in a baking dish, and make a slit in each piece, lengthwise. Fill the meat mixture into the slit in the eggplant, and garnish it with a slice of tomato.

Combine the balance of the tomato sauce with the water, and pour it into the baking dish. Bake in a 375° F. oven for 45 minutes. Serve with pilaf.

TURLU GUEVEJ / *A lovely potpourri of vegetables and lamb*
6 to 8 servings

3 *tablespoons butter*
1 *pound white onions,*
peeled
½ *leg of lamb, boned and*
cut into 2-inch cubes
1 *clove garlic, finely*
chopped
salt and pepper to taste
1½ *cups water*
1 *small eggplant, cut into*
2-inch cubes

2 *carrots, cut into 1-inch*
slices
2 *medium zucchini, cut into*
1-inch slices
¼ *pound string beans, cut*
in half crosswise
¼ *pound fresh okra or 1*
package frozen okra
½ *cup tomato sauce*

Heat the butter in a saucepan. Add the onions, and braise them until they are golden brown. Remove the onions and set them aside. Sauté the meat in the same saucepan with the remaining butter, turning until the cubes of meat are well browned. Add the chopped garlic to the saucepan and stir for a minute. Season the meat with salt and pepper, and add the water. Cover the saucepan and let the meat simmer for about 1½ hours. This portion of the cooking may be done a day ahead.

Sprinkle the cubed eggplant generously with salt and set aside for 30 minutes. This removes any bitterness the eggplant might have. Rinse the eggplant in cold water to remove the salt. Arrange the meat evenly around a large and shallow casserole. Add the onions between the pieces of meat. Continue to arrange the other vegetables the same way, so they are equally distributed. Add the tomato sauce to the meat juices in the saucepan and stir. Taste the liquid to make sure the seasoning is right, and pour the liquid into the casserole over the vegetables and meat. Cover the casserole with either a cover or a piece of aluminum foil, and bake in a 400° F. oven for 30 minutes. Remove the cover and bake for another 30 minutes. Serve immediately with rice or bulghour pilaf.

DUEZMAH / *Eggplant and meat casserole*

6 servings

2 *large eggplants*	*salt and pepper to taste*
3 *pounds chopped lamb*	½ *cup tomato sauce*
1 *medium-size onion,*	½ *cup water*
finely chopped	1 *teaspoon sugar*
½ *cup parsley, finely*	
chopped	

Wash the eggplants, cut the stem end off, and slice crosswise ⅜ inch thick. Sprinkle the slices generously with salt and set aside for 1 hour. Combine the meat, onion, parsley, salt and pepper in a mixing bowl. Mix the ingredients with your hands until they are well blended. Shape the mixture into flat patties about the size of the eggplant slices. Rinse the slices of eggplant with cold water to remove the excess salt. Arrange the eggplant and patties standing up alternately in a casserole. Mix the tomato sauce, water, sugar, and a little salt to taste. Pour the liquid over the eggplant and meat. Cover the casserole and bake in a 400° F. oven for 45 minutes. Serve with bulghour pilaf.

KOUZOU KZARTMA / *One of the many Armenian baked lamb dishes*

6 servings

3 *pounds unboned*
   shoulder of lamb cut
   into 6 serving pieces
1½ *cups water*

½ *cup tomato sauce*
salt and pepper to taste
6 *medium-sized potatoes cut*
   into thick slices

Wash the meat and trim any extra fat. Place it in a casserole and add the water, tomato sauce, and seasoning. Cover and bake in a 400° F. oven for 1 hour.

Remove the cover from the casserole, add the potatoes, and continue to bake the dish uncovered for 1 hour more. Turn the meat and potatoes occasionally to brown them on all sides. Add water as needed.

MEESOV PAGHLAH / *Fava bean stew*

3 to 4 servings

2 *tablespoons butter*
1½ *pounds shoulder of*
   lamb, cut for stew
1 *large onion, sliced*
1½ *teaspoons salt*
⅛ *teaspoon black pepper*

2 *cups water*
1 *pound fava beans*
1 *tablespoon fresh dill,*
   chopped
½ *cup tomato sauce*
1 *teaspoon sugar*

Melt the butter in a saucepan, and sauté the meat in the butter until it browns. Add the onion and sauté the onion as you stir the mixture. Add the salt and pepper, and the water. Cover the saucepan and cook over a low flame for 1½ hours, stirring occasionally.

Wash the fava beans, remove the strings, and cut into 2-inch pieces. Combine the fava beans, dill, tomato sauce, and sugar with the meat in the saucepan. Stir the ingredients and simmer over a low flame for 30 to 35 minutes. Serve with pilaf.

MEESOV BAMIYA / *Lamb and okra stew*

4 servings

3 *tablespoons butter*	*1½ cups water*
2 *pounds boneless lamb,*	*½ cup tomato sauce*
cut into 2-inch cubes	*1 pound fresh okra, or 2*
1 large onion, sliced	*packages frozen okra*
salt and pepper to taste	

Melt the butter in a saucepan, and add the meat and onion. Season the mixture with salt and pepper. Turn occasionally until the meat is well browned. Add the water, and bring the mixture to a boil. Cover the saucepan and simmer on a low flame for 1¼ hours. Add the tomato sauce.

If you have fresh okra, trim the stem end of the okra by removing a cone-shaped portion from the top, being careful not to cut the pod. Wash the okra and combine it with the meat in the saucepan. Mix the meat and okra together and cover the saucepan. Simmer for 30 minutes longer. Serve with rice pilaf.

MEESOV FASSOULIA / *String bean stew*

4 servings

3 *tablespoons butter*	1 *teaspoon salt*
2 *pounds boneless lamb,*	⅛ *teaspoon black pepper*
cut into 2-inch cubes	1 *large onion, sliced*
(or any part of shoul-	1½ *cups water*
der of lamb cut up for	½ *cup tomato sauce*
stew)	1 *pound string beans*

Melt the butter in a saucepan and add the meat. Season with the salt and pepper. Mix occasionally until the meat is browned on all sides. Add the onion and cook for a few minutes longer, until the onion is transparent. Add the water and bring the mixture to a boil. Cover the saucepan and simmer over a low flame for 1¼ hours. Add the tomato sauce and the string beans, which have been washed and cut French style, to the meat in the saucepan. Mix the ingredients together and cover the saucepan. Simmer for 30 minutes longer. Serve with rice pilaf.

PANCHAREGHEN

(VEGETABLES)

BAMIYA / *Okra stew*

4 to 6 servings

1 *pound fresh okra or 2*
   packages frozen okra
1 *large onion, sliced*
3 *tablespoons butter*

½ *cup tomato sauce*
1 *cup water*
1 *teaspoon salt*
⅛ *teaspoon black pepper*

Wash the okra, if fresh, and remove the stem by cutting a cone-shaped layer off. Combine the onion and butter in a saucepan. Sauté the onion until it is soft and just beginning to brown. Add the tomato sauce, water, salt and pepper, and the okra. Cover the saucepan and cook over a low flame for ½ hour. Serve as a side dish with lamb and pilaf.

HAVGITOV FASSOULIA / *String bean omelet*

6 servings

1 *pound string beans*
1½ *quarts water, salted*
1 *large onion, chopped*

2 *tablespoons butter*
4 *eggs*
½ *cup tomato sauce*

Remove the strings of the beans by snapping off both ends. Wash the beans and cut them down the center in French style.

Put 1½ quarts of water into a saucepan and bring the water to a boil. Add the beans and 1 tablespoon of salt to the water, and bring them to a boil again. Then cover the saucepan, lower the flame and simmer until the beans are just tender and green. Do not overcook them.

Combine the onion and butter in a skillet. Sauté the onion until it is transparent. Drain the cooked beans and add them to the onion. Turn the mixture into a buttered baking dish.

Beat the eggs with the tomato sauce, and pour over the bean mixture in the baking dish. Mix them. Bake the bean mixture in a 400° F. oven for 40 to 45 minutes, until the eggs are set and the top is lightly browned. Serve as a side dish.

FASSOULIA SALATA / *String bean salad*

6 servings

1 *pound string beans*
2 *quarts water, salted*
1 *onion, sliced*
salt
2 *large tomatoes*
½ *cup parsley, finely chopped*
¼ *cup fresh dill, finely chopped*
2 *tablespoons vinegar*
¼ *cup olive oil*

Wash the beans in cold water and break the tip off both ends. Cut the beans into pieces about 2 inches long. Drop the beans into boiling, salted water, cover the saucepan, and cook them until they are just tender. Do not overcook them. Drain the beans and set them aside to cool.

Combine the sliced onion in a mixing bowl with a tablespoon of salt (to release the strong onion juices). Crush the onion with the heel of your hand. When the onion has become limp, rinse the slices in cold water to remove all the salt and the onion juices. Cut the tomatoes into small pieces, and combine them in the mixing bowl with the onions. Add the chopped parsley, chopped dill, the cooled beans, 1 teaspoon salt, the vinegar and olive oil. Mix and serve.

TOMATESOV SALATA / *Tomato salad*

6 servings

2 *large onions*
salt to taste
6 *large ripe but firm tomatoes*

1 large green pepper
1 cup chopped parsley
olive oil and vinegar to taste

Slice the onions and place them in a mixing bowl. Sprinkle them very generously with salt. Crush the onions with the salt, stirring and crushing with the heel of your hand until the juices of the onion are released. Then rinse the onions well to remove the salt. Wash the tomatoes, cut them into bite-size pieces, and add them to the onions. Slice the green pepper into the mixture. Add the parsley and mix the ingredients. Season to taste with salt, olive oil, and vinegar.

BABA GHANOUSH / *Eggplant salad*

4 servings

1 large eggplant
1 large tomato
1 small onion, finely chopped
1 small green pepper, finely chopped

½ cup parsley, finely chopped
1½ teaspoons salt
1½ teaspoons vinegar
4 teaspoons olive oil

Wash the eggplant, place it in a baking dish, and put under the broiler. When the skin of the eggplant facing the flame becomes charred, turn it, and continue until all sides are well charred. Remove the pan and set aside. When the eggplant is cool enough to handle, slit the top, scoop out the pulp with a spoon, and place it into a bowl. Discard the skin. Chop the pulp with a knife until it is partially mashed. Cut the tomato into small pieces, and add it to the eggplant with the chopped onion, green pepper, and parsley. Add the salt, vinegar, and olive oil, and mix well. Chill.

BULGHOUROV SPANAKH / *Spinach and bulghour*

6 servings

¾ *stick butter*
2 *large onions, finely chopped*
3½ *cups water*

¾ *cup large bulghour*
2½ *teaspoons salt*
1 *pound spinach*
⅛ *teaspoon black pepper*

Melt the butter in a skillet, and add the chopped onions. Sauté the onions until they are well browned. Set aside.

Combine the water, bulghour, and salt in a saucepan. Cover the saucepan and cook over a moderate flame for 15 minutes. Wash the spinach thoroughly to be sure all sand has been washed out. Add the spinach, the contents of the skillet, and the black pepper to the bulghour mixture in the saucepan. Cover, and simmer over a low flame for 15 minutes. Serve hot, as a side dish in small deep dishes.

HAVGITOV SPANAKH / *Spinach omelet*

6 servings

1 *pound spinach*
1½ *teaspoons salt*
⅛ *teaspoon black pepper*

1 *tablespoon flour*
4 *eggs*
5 *tablespoons butter*

Wash the spinach thoroughly, and cut it up coarsely into a mixing bowl. Add the salt, pepper, flour, and eggs to the bowl. Stir the ingredients well.

Put 3 tablespoons of butter into an omelet pan. Melt the butter and tilt the pan from side to side to coat the sides of the pan. Pour the spinach mixture into the pan, and lower the flame. Shake the pan back and forth to prevent sticking. When the egg is set and lightly browned on the bottom, place a plate over the pan as a cover, and turn the pan upside down. Put the balance of the butter into the pan, over a low flame. Slip the uncooked side of the omelet into the pan, and continue to shake the pan to prevent sticking. When the egg is set and lightly browned, remove the omelet by placing a plate again on the top of the pan and turning it upside down. Cut into pie-shaped wedges.

MADZOONOV SPANAKH / *Spinach with madzoon*

5 to 6 servings

1 pound spinach   *2 cups madzoon*
½ teaspoon salt

Cut off the tough stems and roots of the spinach, and discard them. Wash the spinach several times until it is free of all sand. Lift the spinach from the water with your hands and place it into a saucepan, without any additional water. Add the salt, cover the saucepan, and cook over moderate heat for 5 to 6 minutes. Drain the spinach well and set aside to cool. Stir the madzoon in a bowl with a spoon until it is smooth. Add the cooled spinach to the bowl and mix it with the madzoon. Serve cold.

TUTUMOV BOERAG / *Baked zucchini pie*

6 to 8 servings

4 *medium-sized zucchini*	½ *cup flour*
4 *eggs*	1 *teaspoon salt*
1 *cup muenster cheese,*	⅛ *teaspoon pepper*
grated	4 *tablespoons butter*
¼ *cup chopped parsley*	

Wash the zucchini thoroughly and grate them into a mixing bowl. Sprinkle the grated zucchini lightly with salt, and set them aside for 10 to 15 minutes. (The salt will draw out some liquid.) Take a handful of the zucchini in your hand and squeeze it to remove as much of the liquid as you can. Continue until all of the zucchini is drained. Combine the zucchini with the eggs, muenster cheese, parsley, flour, and salt and pepper. Mix thoroughly. Pour the mixture into a buttered 10 × 10-inch baking dish. Dot with the butter. Bake in a 375° F. oven for 45 minutes. Serve hot.

PANDJARABOUR / *Swiss chard stew*

6 servings

1 *bunch Swiss chard*	1⅓ *cups yellow lentils*
⅔ *cup gorgod*	¼ *pound butter*
7 *cups water, salted*	3 *large onions, chopped*

Wash the Swiss chard and remove the stems. Put the gorgod in a large saucepan with 7 cups of water seasoned with salt. Bring the water to a boil, then lower the flame and simmer the gorgod for 1½ hours. When the gorgod is almost tender, wash and add the yellow lentils. Simmer the mixture for about ½ hour, stirring occasionally to avoid lumps. Add the Swiss chard and continue cooking the mixture until the Swiss chard is tender.

Heat the butter in a skillet. Add the onions and sauté them until they are golden brown. Empty the contents of the skillet into the Swiss chard mixture and stir. Serve the pandjarabour hot.

pilaf (RICE AND CRACKED WHEAT)

Pilaf is the Armenian staple. It is made with rice or bulghour and it comes in a variety of forms—simple or elegant, but always delicious.

PRINZOV PILAF / *Pilaf made with rice and noodles*

4 servings

⅛ *pound butter*
½ *cup fine egg noodles*
1 *cup rice (long grain is preferable)*

2 *cups hot chicken broth*
salt to taste

Melt the butter in a saucepan and add the egg noodles. Stir the noodles and butter constantly until the noodles turn golden in color. Add the rice to the ingredients and mix. Add the hot chicken broth and salt. Bring the liquid to a boil, then lower the flame as much as possible. Cover the saucepan and let the pilaf simmer slowly until the liquid has been absorbed.

DONN ORVA PILAF / *Pilaf made with currants and pine nuts*

8 servings

¼ *pound butter*
2 *cups rice*
4 *cups chicken broth*
½ *cup currants*

½ *cup pine nuts*
½ *teaspoon allspice*
salt and pepper to taste

Melt the butter in a saucepan. Add the rice and stir for a minute. Add the hot chicken broth, currants, pine nuts, and seasonings and mix all the ingredients. Bring the liquid to a boil. Lower the flame and cover the saucepan. Simmer the pilaf slowly until the liquid is absorbed.

This pilaf is particularly good served with roast capon.

NOUSHOV PILAF / *Pilaf made with kidneys and almonds*

8 servings

8 lamb kidneys	2 cups rice
¼ pound butter	4 cups chicken broth
salt and pepper to taste	½ cup blanched almonds

Cut the kidneys into ½-inch pieces, making sure to remove the tough white center. Melt in a skillet one third of the butter. Season the kidneys with salt and pepper and sauté, stirring occasionally until they have browned.

Heat the balance of the butter in a saucepan and add the rice to it. Stir the rice with the butter for a minute or two, then add the hot chicken broth, salt and pepper to taste, the almonds, and the kidneys along with the butter and particles left in the skillet. Bring the liquid to a boil and then lower the flame and cover the saucepan. Let the pilaf simmer slowly until the liquid is absorbed.

This is an elegant accompaniment for turkey.

TOMATESOV PILAF / *Another rice pilaf*

4 servings

⅛ pound butter	2 cups meat broth
1 cup rice	salt to taste
½ cup tomato sauce	

Melt the butter in a saucepan and add the rice. Stir over a low flame for a minute or two. Remove.

Combine the tomato sauce, the hot meat broth, and the salt in another saucepan and bring them to a boil. Add the hot liquid to the rice and bring it to a boil again. Lower the flame as much as possible and cover the saucepan. Simmer gently until the liquid is absorbed and the rice is fluffy.

BULGHOUR PILAF

4 servings

⅛ pound butter	2 cups lamb broth
½ cup fine egg noodles	1 teaspoon sweet basil
1 cup large bulghour	salt and pepper to taste

Melt the butter in a saucepan and add the egg noodles. Stir the mixture constantly until the noodles are golden brown. Add the bulghour to the noodles and stir for another minute. Add the hot lamb broth, the basil, and salt and pepper to taste, and bring the liquid to a boil. Lower the flame as much as possible and simmer the pilaf slowly until the bulghour has absorbed all of the liquid.

MUEDJATDERA / *Pilaf made with lentils*

6 servings

1 cup lentils	salt and pepper to taste
2 cups water, salted	2 medium onions, chopped
2 cups broth	¾ stick of butter
1 cup large bulghour	

Wash the lentils and add the water salted to taste. Bring it to a rolling boil for 1 to 2 minutes and drain. Bring the broth to a boil and add the drained lentils, the bulghour, and the seasoning.

Bring the pot to a boil again, lower the flame as much as possible, cover the pot and let the mixture simmer until the liquid is absorbed.

Fry the chopped onions in the butter until they are lightly browned. Add them to the lentils and bulghour and stir gently with a fork.

khumoreghen

(BREADS AND PASTRIES)

LAVASH / *Armenian flat bread. The Armenians love to make sandwiches of the soft lavash, which they wrap around various fillings such as kebabs, hummos, cheeses, etc.*

8 lavash

8 *cups flour*
1½ *tablespoons salt*
1 *tablespoon sugar*
1 *package yeast dissolved in ½ cup lukewarm water*

2 *cups warm water*
¼ *pound melted warm butter*

Combine the flour, salt, and sugar in a large mixing bowl. Make a well in the center and pour in the yeast, water, and the melted butter. Blend the ingredients with your hands. Knead the dough for about 5 minutes. Cover the bowl with waxed paper and a kitchen towel. Put a sweater over the towel to keep the dough warm. Set it aside for 3 hours.

Uncover the dough and divide it into 8 pieces. Roll each piece into a ball. Sprinkle some flour on a corner of the table and line up the balls of dough on the flour. Cover them with a towel and let them rest for 10 minutes.

Sprinkle flour on the table, place a ball of dough on the flour, and roll the dough with a rolling pin to a diameter of 15 inches. Take a fork and prick the rolled-out dough all over. Preheat the oven to 375° F.

Make a rolling pin from a dowel that is 1 inch in diameter and a yard long. Place the dowel over the center of the rolled-out dough and fold half of the dough over the dowel. Pick up the dowel with the dough over it and spread the dough gently on the floor of your oven. Bake the lavash for about 2 minutes until it bubbles evenly over the surface and the bottom begins to brown slightly. Watch it constantly to prevent burning. When the underside of the bread is lightly browned, pick it up with a spatula in one hand and a potholder in the other and put it in the broiler to brown the top lightly for a few seconds. This bread is eaten either crisp or soft. To soften the lavash run it under water on both sides, shake the water off, and wrap it in a towel for ½ hour.

PIDEH / *Armenian bread*

2 loaves

4 *cups flour*
¾ *tablespoon salt*
½ *tablespoon sugar*
⅛ *pound warm melted butter*

1 *cup warm milk*
1 *package yeast dissolved in ½ cup warm water*
more melted butter

Combine the dry ingredients in a large mixing bowl. Make a well in the center and pour in all of the warm liquid ingredients, mixed. Blend the liquid and dry ingredients with your hands, then knead the dough for about 5 minutes. Cover the bowl with wax paper and a towel over the paper. Add a sweater to keep the dough warm. Set it aside to rest for 1½ hours. Uncover the dough, knead it again for a couple of minutes, cover it again, and let it rest for another 1½ hours.

When the dough has risen again, divide it in half. Roll each piece in the shape of a ball and flatten the balls with a rolling pin to about 8 inches in diameter by 1 inch thick. Place each piece in a buttered pan. Brush the tops of the dough with melted butter, cover them again, and set them in a warm place to rise again for 1 hour.

Preheat the oven to 375° F. Bake the bread for about 45 minutes or until the loaves are golden brown.

KATAH / *A flaky breakfast pastry that is good at any time served with coffee and cheese*

22 buns

2 packages yeast
½ cup water, lukewarm
7½ cups flour
2 tablespoons sugar
2 tablespoons salt
1 tablespoon baking powder
3 eggs, room temperature

½ pound butter, melted and lukewarm
1½ cups milk, lukewarm
1 pound melted butter to brush on dough
2 eggs, beaten
½ cup sesame seeds
1 teaspoon black caraway seeds

Combine the yeast with the water in a small bowl and set it aside to dissolve.

Combine all of the dry ingredients in a large mixing bowl. Make a well in the center and add the eggs, melted butter, milk, and the dissolved yeast. Mix the ingredients by hand and knead until the dough is smooth. Add more flour or warm liquid as needed to make a firm but not stiff dough. Cover the dough with wax paper and a towel over it. Now cover the bowl with a blanket and set it in a warm place for 2 or 3 hours or until the dough has doubled in size.

Cut the dough into 12 pieces and roll each piece into a ball. Sprinkle some flour on a baking sheet and arrange the balls of dough on the flour. Cover with a towel and let the dough rest for 10 minutes.

With a rolling pin roll out each ball of dough until it is 14 to 16 inches in diameter. Brush the surface generously with melted butter. Cut the circle in half and roll each half into a loose rope, then roll the rope into a twisted roll or bun. Set the buns aside to allow the butter to cool as you prepare the rest of the dough in the same manner.

Take each bun and roll it with a rolling pin to an oval shape about ½ inch thick. Arrange the katahs on a baking pan, brush the surface with a beaten egg, and sprinkle with sesame seeds mixed with some black seeds. Set them aside for ½ hour. Bake them in a 400° F. oven for 20 to 25 minutes. Katahs can be frozen and reheated before serving.

KHORITZOV KATAH / *A flaky breakfast pastry with an unbelievable filling*

14 buns

KHORITZ

¼ pound salt butter   1 cup flour

Melt the butter in a skillet. Add the flour and stir the mixture over a low flame for about 5 minutes until the butter and flour are well blended. Set it aside to cool.

DOUGH

1 package yeast	*¼ pound plus 3 tablespoons*
¼ cup water, lukewarm	*butter, melted*
5 cups flour	*1 cup milk, lukewarm*
4 teaspoons sugar	*more melted butter*
4 teaspoons salt	*1 egg, beaten*
1½ teaspoons baking	*½ cup sesame seeds*
powder	*1 teaspoon black caraway*
2 eggs	*seeds*

Combine the yeast and warm water in a small bowl and set it aside to allow the yeast to dissolve.

Combine all of the dry ingredients in a large mixing bowl. Make a well in the center and add 2 eggs, melted butter, the warm milk, and the dissolved yeast. Mix the ingredients by hand and knead until the dough is smooth. Add more flour or warm milk as needed to make a firm but not too stiff dough. Cover the dough with wax paper and a towel over it. Now cover the bowl with a blanket and set it aside for 2 or 3 hours or until the dough has doubled in size.

Cut the dough into 7 pieces. Roll each one into a ball. Sprinkle some flour in a baking pan and place the balls of dough on the flour. Cover the dough with a towel and let it rest for 10 minutes.

With a rolling pin, roll each piece of dough to a diameter of 14 to 16 inches. Brush the surface generously with melted butter. Cut the circle in half and fold each half into a 5-inch square. Set these aside to allow the butter to cool as you roll, butter, and fold the balance of the dough.

Take each folded square, place a tablespoon of khoritz in the center, and fold the square in half over the khoritz. Press along the edges to seal in the filling, and with the rolling pin, roll out the square until it is ½ inch thick.

Arrange the katahs on a baking sheet, brush the surfaces with a beaten egg, and sprinkle them with sesame seeds mixed with black caraway seeds. Bake them in a 400° F. oven for 20 to 25 minutes.

GRANDMA'S SIMIT / *An unsweetened crisp breakfast pastry*
about 100 pastries

I suggest that you prepare this dough in the evening and allow it to rise overnight.

1 package yeast	*1 tablespoon salt*
½ cup lukewarm water	*1¾ cups milk*
1¾ pounds butter,	*3 eggs, room temperature*
melted	*2 eggs, beaten*
4 pounds flour	*sesame seeds*

Dissolve the yeast in the warm water. Melt the butter and cool to tepid. Put the flour and salt in a large mixing bowl, make a well in the center of it, and pour in the butter. Rub the flour and butter together with your hands until they are blended.

Heat the milk until it is warm. Make another well in the flour mixture, add the warm milk, the yeast, and the 3 eggs. Mix the liquid with the flour. Knead the mixture vigorously for about 10 minutes. It will be sticky at first but it will gradually pull away from your hands and the bowl. Form it into a ball in the bowl and make a cross cut on top of the dough with a knife. Cover the bowl

with wax paper and a kitchen towel. Find a clean old blanket or
sweater and bundle the bowl to keep it warm. Let it rest overnight.

The following morning take a handful of the dough and place
it on a table sprinkled with flour. Roll it out with your hands in
the shape of a rope that is about ½ inch thick. Cut the rope into
8-inch lengths, then fold each piece in half and twist once. Place
the simits in a baking pan as you make them. Brush the tops of
the simits with the beaten eggs and sprinkle them with sesame
seeds. Preheat the oven to 375° F. Bake the simits for about 25
minutes until they are golden brown.

The simit is delicious at any time with coffee and it keeps for
weeks.

CHOEREG / *This is a lightly sweetened breakfast bun*

about 60 buns

2 *pounds flour*
1 *teaspoon salt*
¾ *cup sugar*
½ *teaspoon mahleb, ground*
½ *teaspoon anisette seeds, ground*
1 *teaspoon black caraway seeds*

1 *package yeast dissolved in ¼ cup lukewarm water*
3 *eggs, room temperature*
1½ *cups lukewarm melted butter*
1 *cup warm milk*
1 *egg, beaten*
sesame seeds

Combine the flour, salt, sugar, mahleb, anisette seeds, and black
seeds in a large mixing bowl and blend. Make a well in the center
of the dry mixture and pour in the yeast, the 3 eggs, the melted

butter, and the warm milk. Blend the mixture by hand and knead it until the dough seems well blended and stops clinging to your hands and the bowl. Cover the bowl with a piece of wax paper and a kitchen towel. Cover the towel with a sweater or blanket to keep the dough warm. Let the dough rest for about 4 hours.

Take a handful of dough and roll it out on the table into a rope that is about 1¼ inches thick. Cut the rope into 9-inch lengths. Fold each piece in half and twist it once. Place the choeregs on a buttered baking pan. Brush the top of each choereg with the beaten egg and sprinkle it with sesame seeds. Preheat the oven to 375° F. Bake the choeregs for about 25 minutes or until they are golden brown. The choeregs can be frozen and reheated before serving.

BISHI / *Armenian pancakes*

4 to 6 servings

1½ tablespoons melted butter	1½ teaspoons baking powder
½ cup water	½ teaspoon salt
1 egg, beaten	2 tablespoons butter
1½ cups flour	sugar

Combine the liquid ingredients in a mixing bowl and stir. Add the flour, baking powder, and salt. Knead the mixture by hand until the dough is well blended and smooth. Roll the dough into small balls about the size of a walnut. Roll each ball of dough with a rolling pin into a 5- or 6-inch circle.

Melt 2 tablespoons of butter in a small skillet. Sauté the circles of dough in the skillet until they are golden on both sides.

Sprinkle them with sugar while they are hot and serve them immediately. Additional butter should be added to the skillet as needed.

SUSAMOV KHUMOREGHEN / *A crisp, mildly sweet cookie sprinkled with sesame seeds*

about 8 dozen cookies

1 pound butter	*½ pint heavy cream*
1½ cups sugar	*1 teaspoon vanilla*
2 eggs	*2 eggs, beaten*
7½ cups flour	*sesame seeds*
3 teaspoons baking powder	

Cream the butter and sugar until they are light and fluffy. Add the 2 eggs and beat. Gradually add the flour and baking powder alternating with the cream and vanilla. Mix the ingredients with a spoon until the mixture begins to thicken. Then use your hands and knead until the mixture is well blended.

Take a ball of the mixture and roll it out on the table to a rope about ½ inch thick. Cut it into 6-inch lengths. Turn each piece into a pretzel shape and place it on a baking sheet. Brush the top of each piece with the beaten eggs and sprinkle with sesame seeds. Preheat the oven to 400° F. Bake the cookies for about 30 minutes.

UNGOUYZOV KHUMOREGHEN / *Walnut and raisin-filled cookies*

3 dozen cookies

WALNUT AND RAISIN FILLING

½ cup walnuts, finely   ¾ cup sugar
   chopped   1 teaspoon cinnamon
¼ cup raisins

Combine the walnuts, raisins, sugar, and cinnamon in a bowl, mix together, and set aside.

PASTRY

½ pound butter   ⅓ cup milk, or more
2½ cups flour   1 egg, beaten
1 egg

In a mixing bowl, blend the butter and flour with your hands very quickly, until the mixture resembles coarse meal. Add the egg, and sprinkle the milk over the mixture. Blend together, and gather it into a ball. Use a little additional milk if it is needed to hold the dough. As soon as the dough holds together, stop handling it. Divide the dough into 3 portions and roll them into balls. Sprinkle flour lightly onto the table and over one ball of dough. Roll it into a 10-inch circle, and cut it as a pie into 12 slices. Sprinkle generously with the raisin-nut mixture, and roll each slice of dough, starting with the wide end, as a jelly roll. Arrange the cookies on a buttered baking pan. Brush the top of each cookie with a beaten egg. Bake in a 375° F. oven for 30 to 35 minutes.

KHOURABIA / *This is the Armenian version of shortbread*

about 30 cookies

½ pound sweet butter   2 cups flour
1 cup extra fine sugar

Clarify the butter as follows: Melt the butter over a low flame, then set it in the refrigerator until it is cool. Remove the foam from the top of the saucepan, discard the water in the bottom of the saucepan and use only the hardened butter in the middle which is called clarified butter.

Cream the butter with the sugar until it is fluffy and light. Gradually add the flour, kneading the mixture until it is well blended and stops clinging to your fingers.

Take a small portion about the size of a walnut, roll it into an oval shape, place it on the baking sheet, turning it into a crescent shape. Bake in a 350° F. oven for 25 minutes.

Variation: Stuffed Khourabia

about 25 cookies

FILLING

4 ounces ground walnuts   3 tablespoons sugar and
    mixed with   1 teaspoon cinnamon

Take a portion of the khourabia dough about the size of a walnut and form it into a cone shape. Push your index finger into the center of the dough, pressing gently around the wall to make a hollow. Place a spoonful of the nut mixture in the hollow. Seal the opening gently by pushing the outer shell together again. Pat it very carefully into a flattened ball. Place it on a baking sheet.

Continue making the balance of the khourabias. Bake in a 350° F. oven for 25 minutes.

This is a dessert that truly "melts in the mouth."

PAKHLAVA *(with rolled dough)* / *A flaky, many-layered, nut-pastry*

48 pastries

FILLING

4 *cups walnuts, finely chopped*	½ *cup sugar*
	3 *teaspoons cinnamon*

Combine the above ingredients in a mixing bowl, blend them, and set them aside.

SYRUP

2 *cups sugar*	1 *tablespoon lemon juice*
1½ *cups water*	

Combine the sugar and water in a saucepan. Boil the liquid for 8 minutes. Add the lemon juice and boil for 2 minutes longer. Set the syrup aside to cool.

PASTRY

4 *cups flour*	4 *tablespoons olive oil*
1 *teaspoon salt*	1 *cup water*
1 *teaspoon baking powder*	1 *box cornstarch*
2 *eggs*	1½ *pound sweet butter, melted*

Combine the flour, salt, and baking powder in a mixing bowl and make a well in the center. Add the eggs, 2 tablespoons of olive oil, and the water. Knead the mixture by hand, dipping your hands lightly into the balance of the oil, for 10 minutes. Cut the dough into 20 equal parts. Roll each piece into a smooth ball, dip a finger into the oil, and coat the ball of dough lightly to prevent the dough from crusting. Dip the oiled ball lightly into the cornstarch and place it in a baking pan. When all the balls of dough have been prepared, cover the pan with a dry towel, then put a damp towel over it. Set the pan aside to rest for 2 hours.

Sprinkle some cornstarch lightly on the table, place a ball of dough on it, and with a rolling pin, roll it out to an 8-inch circle. Roll 4 more balls of dough into 8-inch circles and stack the 5 circles with a heaping tablespoonful of cornstarch evenly spread between each layer. Roll out the 5 circles together to a 15-inch diameter. Now use a long 1-inch dowel to continue rolling the circles. Place the dowel over the stack of 5 circles 1 inch from the bottom edge. Fold the lower edge over the dowel and roll it to the end of the circles, pressing gently as you roll. Flip the outer layer of dough over the dowel away from you and unroll the stack. This procedure will displace the outer layer so that in the next rolling it will fall on the inside of the stack, and there will be a new outer layer to flip away and displace. Continue rolling, flipping, and unrolling the layers until each of the 5 layers has moved from an outside position to an inside position. This is done not only to roll them paper-thin but to make sure that the layers are not sticking to one another. If necessary a little cornstarch may be added between layers to prevent sticking. The sheets should be approximately 30 inches in diameter when you have completed rolling them. Fold the sheets into quarters, wrap in wax paper, and set aside.

Roll out the balance of the dough in stacks of 5 the same way.

Open one stack of dough at a time and spread the dough flat on the table. Place a circular baking pan (2 inches deep by 16 inches in diameter) over the 5-layer stack and cut the layers around the pan with a knife, using the pan as a pattern. (Save the pieces of dough that have been cut away.) Place a layer in the pan, brush it lightly with butter, and continue placing one layer over the next with melted butter over each layer. Arrange the extra pieces of dough between the 5 layers and butter them. When the layers have been placed in the pan, sprinkle a layer of the nut mixture over them. Open another package of dough and proceed as you did with the last package, and sprinkle a layer of nut mixture over it. Continue with the balance of the dough. There will be a total of about 30 to 35 layers of pastry including the extra pieces, with 3 layers of nuts in between the sets of dough.

Cut through the layers with a sharp knife into 2-inch strips across the pan. Now cut diagonally into diamond-shaped pieces. There will be about 48 pieces of pakhlava.

Place the pan in a preheated 375° F. oven. Bake the pakhlava for 10 minutes, pull the pan out, and add a tablespoonful of hot butter between each piece. This will make the layers of pastry puff up. Continue baking for 35 minutes longer. Remove the pan from the oven and tilt it over a container to remove the excess butter.

Put a tablespoonful of cooled syrup on each piece of pakhlava while it is still hot. Pick the pan up, tilt it from side to side to make sure each piece is evenly coated with syrup. Drain out the excess syrup in the bottom of the pan to prevent sogginess. Serve when cool.

BANIROV PAKHLAVA / *Rolled pakhlava dough with cheese filling*

36 pastries

1 recipe pakhlava pastry
1½ pounds Armenian
    cheese

1 pound sweet butter, melted

SYRUP

2 cups sugar
1½ cups water

1 tablespoon lemon juice

Combine the sugar and water in a saucepan. Boil the mixture for 8 minutes. Add the lemon juice and boil for 2 minutes longer. Set the syrup aside to cool.

Prepare the pastry sheets as described on pages 98–100. Place 10 layers of pastry, one at a time, in a 12 × 16-inch baking pan. Be sure to brush the surface of each layer with melted butter as you place it in the pan.

Cut the cheese into ½-inch slices. Arrange the pieces of cheese close together over the 10 layers of pastry.

Add 10 more layers of pastry over the cheese brushing the surface of each layer with melted butter. Cut through the layers with a sharp knife, dividing the pastry into 3-inch square pieces. Bake in a preheated 375° F. oven. Bake the pakhlava for 10 minutes, pull the pan out, add a tablespoonful of hot butter between each square. This will puff the pastry up as it bakes. Continue the baking for another 35 minutes. Remove the pan and tilt it over a container to remove all the excess butter.

Put a tablespoonful of the cooled syrup over each piece of pakhlava while it is hot. Tilt the pan from side to side to be sure each piece is well coated with the syrup. Drain out the excess syrup to prevent sogginess. Serve warm.

PAKHLAVA (*with pulled dough*) / *A flaky, many-layered, nut-filled pastry*

about 40 pastries

FILLING

1 *pound walnuts, ground*   3 *teaspoons cinnamon*
3 *tablespoons sugar*

Combine the walnuts, sugar, and cinnamon in a mixing bowl and set aside.

SYRUP

4 *cups sugar*   2 *teaspoons lemon juice*
3 *cups water*

Combine the sugar and water in a saucepan. Bring the mixture to a boil, lower the flame, and simmer for 10 minutes. Add the lemon juice and simmer for 1 minute longer. Set aside to cool.

DOUGH

6⅔ *cups flour*   1 *egg*
pinch of salt   3 *tablespoons melted butter*
2 *teaspoons baking*   2¼ *cups warm water*
    powder   2 *pounds clarified butter*

Combine all of the dry ingredients in a large mixing bowl. Make a well in the center, add the egg, the 3 tablespoons butter, and the warm water. Knead the mixture by hand for 15 minutes. The dough should not stick to your hands or the bowl but should be smooth and silky. Divide the dough into 4 equal portions. Roll each piece to resemble a French bread and cut it into 16 pieces. Roll each of the cut pieces into a smooth ball. Sprinkle flour lightly on the table, and place the balls 1 inch apart on the flour. Cover the 64 balls of dough with a dry towel and place a damp towel over them. Cover the damp towel with a terry towel to keep the dough warm, and let it rest for 30 minutes.

Sprinkle some cornstarch lightly on the table, take one piece of dough at a time, place it on the cornstarch, and sprinkle it as well. Roll the dough with a rolling pin to a 6-inch circle. Brush the top and bottom of the circle lightly with cornstarch again, and set it aside. Continue rolling the balls out until you have 32 circles, each brushed with cornstarch. Place one circle over another into two stacks of 16 circles each. Place a towel over the circles to keep them from drying out.

Butter a 12 × 16-inch baking pan.

Pick up the first circle gently. Hold the circle upright along the edge with your fingers turning and stretching it as you turn it. When the circle gets larger make a fist with each hand and hold it under the sheet of dough. Stretch your arms apart gently as the dough stretches. When the dough is as thin as tissue paper place it over the side of the baking pan and stretch the sheet across the pan. Adjust the sheet of dough on all sides of the pan stretching it as much as possible without tearing it. Let the edges of dough hang over the sides of the pan to be trimmed away later. Brush the layer of dough generously and carefully with melted butter.

Stretch, place, and butter the rest of the 32 layers as you did the first. Spread the nut mixture evenly over the first 32 layers of dough.

Repeat with the other 32 balls of dough placing them over the layer of nuts so there will be 64 sheets of dough in the pan with a layer of nuts in the middle.

Trim away the edges of dough hanging over the sides of the pan. Cut the pakhlava into 10 horizontal strips and then cut diagonally across them to make diamond-shaped pieces.

Bake the pakhlava in a preheated 400° F. oven for 10 minutes. Heat the balance of the butter until it is very hot, but not browned. Pour a tablespoon of butter on each diamond in the pan. Lower the oven temperature to 350° F. and bake the pakhlava for another 45 minutes. Drain as much of the butter from the pan as possible. Tilt the pan for 10 minutes and remove any butter left in the pan.

Add a tablespoon of the cooled syrup to each piece of pakhlava.

Serve at room temperature.

For special guests!

PAKHLAVA (with filo) / Pakhlava the easy way!

40 pastries

1 pound filo

1 pound sweet butter, melted

SYRUP

1½ cups water

2 cups sugar

2 teaspoons lemon juice

Combine the sugar and water in a saucepan. Cook them over a moderate flame for 8 minutes. Add the lemon juice. Cook for 2 minutes longer and set aside to cool.

FILLING

1 pound shelled and ground walnuts	*½ cup sugar* *3 teaspoons cinnamon*

Combine the ground walnuts, sugar, and cinnamon in a small bowl and mix them until they are evenly blended.

Open the package of filo and lay the sheets on the table in a stack. Cover the surface with a dry towel and then a damp towel over it to prevent the sheets of dough from drying out.

Spread one sheet of dough in an 11 × 16-inch buttered baking pan. Spread the surface of the sheet of dough with melted butter. Take another sheet and place it over the first sheet and brush it with butter. Repeat the process until half the sheets have been used. Sprinkle the walnut mixture liberally over the entire surface, then continue putting one sheet of dough over the next in the pan with butter brushed over the surface of each until the balance of dough has been used.

Cut the pastry with a sharp knife into 2-inch strips, then cut again diagonally into diamond shapes.

Bake in a 375° F. oven for 20 minutes. If there is any butter left, heat it and pour it over the surface while the pakhlava is baking. Lower the temperature to 250° F. and bake the pakhlava for 1 hour and 10 minutes longer. Remove the pan from the oven and tilt it over a container to drain off as much of the butter as possible. Pour a tablespoonful of the cool syrup over each diamond. Allow the pakhlava to cool before serving.

BOURMA / *Rolled, shirred filo in syrup with a nut filling*

50 pastries

> *1 pound filo*
> *1½ pounds sweet butter,*
>   *melted*

SYRUP

> *1½ cups water*   *2 teaspoons lemon juice*
> *2 cups sugar*

Combine the water and sugar in a saucepan. Cook the mixture for 8 minutes. Add the lemon juice. Cook for an additional 2 minutes. Set aside to cool.

FILLING

> *1 pound shelled walnuts,*   *½ cup sugar*
>   *ground*   *2 teaspoons cinnamon*

Combine the ground walnuts, sugar, and cinnamon in a bowl. Mix them until they are evenly blended.

Open the package of filo and spread it out flat on the table. Cover the surface with a dry towel with a damp towel over it to prevent the dough from drying. Take one sheet of dough at a time and be sure to cover the balance with the towel each time. Spread the sheet on the table and sprinkle a tablespoon of the nut mixture over the sheet. Use a long ¾-inch dowel as a rolling pin. Place the dowel across the wide end of the sheet nearest you. Fold the sheet over the dowel and roll it loosely to the other end. Hold your hands over the rolled sheet and gently push both ends to the center as you might close an accordion. Pull the dowel out carefully and place the bourma on a baking sheet. Cut the bourma in half to make two shorter pieces. Prepare the rest of the bourma. Put a tablespoon of melted butter over each bourma in the pan. Bake them in a 350° F. oven for 20 to 25 minutes. Remove the pan from the oven and pour off as much of the butter as possible. Put a tablespoonful of the cooled syrup over each bourma. Allow them to cool before serving.

KADAYIF / *A pastry of shredded dough with a walnut filling*

8 to 10 servings

SYRUP

2 *cups sugar*
1½ *cups water*

2 *teaspoons lemon juice*

Combine the sugar and water in a saucepan. Bring the mixture to a boil, and lower the flame. Simmer for 10 minutes, and add the lemon juice. Cook 1 minute longer and set aside to cool.

PASTRY

1 *pound kadayif*
2 *cups walnuts, finely chopped*
3 *teaspoons cinnamon*

3 *tablespoons sugar*
½ *pound sweet butter, melted*

Remove any lumpy bits of dough from the kadayif. Arrange half of the kadayif in a 9 × 12-inch baking pan. Mix the chopped walnuts, cinnamon, and sugar together in a bowl. Spread the nut mixture evenly over the kadayif. Arrange the balance of the kadayif evenly over the nuts, pressing down gently with your hand, to smooth the top. Add the hot, melted butter 1 tablespoon at a time, evenly over the entire surface of the kadayif. Cover the pan securely with a sheet of aluminum foil. This will help to keep the kadayif soft. Bake in a 350° F. oven for ½ hour. Uncover the pan and bake for another ½ hour, to a golden brown. Remove the pan from the oven and pour the cooled syrup evenly over the hot kadayif. Cover the pan again with aluminum foil for ½ hour, to keep it moist. Cut into squares and serve.

BANIROV KADAYIF / *A pastry of shredded dough with a cheese filling*

8 to 10 servings

SYRUP

2 *cups sugar*
1½ *cups water*

2 *teaspoons lemon juice*

Combine the sugar and water in a saucepan. Bring the mixture to a boil, and lower the flame. Simmer the mixture for 10 minutes, and add the lemon juice. Cook 1 minute longer, and set aside to cool.

PASTRY

1 *pound kadayif*
½ *pound sweet butter,*
melted

¾ *pound Armenian cheese*
¾ *pound ricotta*

Place the kadayif in a mixing bowl and separate the shreds, removing any lumpy bits of dough. Sprinkle the melted butter over the kadayif, and blend them together with your hands to make sure the shreds are evenly coated. Arrange half of this mixture in a 9 × 12-inch baking dish. Crumble the Armenian cheese, and mix it with the ricotta. Spread the cheese mixture evenly over the layer of kadayif. Arrange the balance of the kadayif over the cheese, pressing down gently with your hand to smooth the top. Cover the baking dish with a sheet of aluminum foil, and bake in a 350° F. oven for ½ hour. Uncover the baking dish and bake for another ½ hour. The kadayif should be golden brown. Remove the baking dish from the oven, and pour the cooled syrup evenly over the hot kadayif. Cover the dish again with aluminum foil for ½ hour, to keep it moist. Cut into squares and serve warm.

EKMEK KADAYIF / *A heavenly dessert that is served with khaimakh (cream)*

4 servings

4 Holland rusk   *½ cup water*

SYRUP

2 cups sugar   *juice of ½ lemon*
1½ cups water

Combine the sugar and water in a saucepan, and boil the mixture for 8 minutes. Add the lemon juice to the syrup and boil 2 minutes longer.

Moisten the Holland rusk with the water. Arrange the moistened rusk in a buttered baking pan just large enough to hold them comfortably. Pour the hot syrup over the rusk. Bake in a preheated oven at 375° F. for 40 to 45 minutes. Cool before serving. Top each serving with a slice of khaimakh.

KHAIMAKH / *A delicious cream topping for ekmek kadayif and other sweets*

10 to 12 servings

1 quart of heavy cream

Pour the cream into a 9-inch-square cake pan, and place over the flame with asbestos in between. Bring the cream to a boil over a very low flame, to prevent scorching. Lift a ladleful of cream up, and pour it from as high as possible back into the pan. This will form bubbles. Continue this procedure, lifting the ladle and pouring it back, for 1 hour. Turn off the fire, and let the cream set for 3 hours.

After 3 hours, set the pan carefully in the refrigerator and leave overnight.

To remove the khaimakh, cut around the four sides of the pan with a knife. Cut into 3 strips, lift each strip gently with a spatula, and roll it up as a jelly roll. Slice when serving.

REVANI / *Farina nut cake soaked in syrup, which gives it the consistency of a rum cake*

8 to 10 servings

SYRUP

4 cups sugar   *5 cups water*

Combine sugar and water in a saucepan and bring the mixture to a boil. Lower the flame, and let the syrup boil for 20 minutes. Set aside to cool.

BATTER

1 *cup farina*
1 *cup flour*
1 *cup sugar*
2 *teaspoons baking powder*

5 *eggs, beaten*
½ *pound butter, melted*
1 *cup chopped walnuts*

Preheat the oven to 375° F. Combine the farina, flour, sugar, and baking powder in a mixing bowl. Add the beaten eggs and the melted butter and beat with an electric mixer. Add the chopped nuts, and mix. Pour into a buttered 9 × 9-inch baking pan. Place the pan in the oven and lower the temperature to 350° F. Bake for 45 minutes. When you remove the pan from the oven, while the revani is still hot cut it into diamond-shaped serving pieces, and pour half of the cooled syrup evenly over the entire surface. Pour the balance of the syrup over the cake 1 hour before serving.

JEVISLI / *Nut-filled cookies*

3 dozen cookies

NUT FILLING

¾ *cup walnuts, finely chopped*

¾ *cup sugar*
1 *teaspoon cinnamon*

Combine the walnuts, sugar, and cinnamon in a bowl, mix them together, and set the bowl aside.

PASTRY

½ pound butter   1 egg
2½ cups flour   ⅓ cup milk, or more

In a mixing bowl, blend the butter and flour with your hands, very quickly, until the mixture resembles a coarse meal. Add the egg, and sprinkle the milk over the mixture. Blend together, and when the dough holds together, gather it into a ball. Use a little additional milk if it is needed. Divide the dough into two portions. Sprinkle flour lightly onto the table. Place one portion of dough on the floured table and sprinkle a little flour on the dough. Roll the dough into ⅛ inch thickness, and cut it into 2 × 4-inch pieces. Pick up one piece at a time and place it in the palm of your hand. Add a teaspoonful of the nut mixture across the length of the dough. Roll the dough over to cover the nut mixture, and seal it. Roll the filled dough gently in the palm of your hands to resemble a small cigar. Arrange the cookies on a buttered baking pan. With a pair of scissors, cut V's across the top of the cookies. Brush the top of the cookies with a beaten egg, and bake in a 375° F. oven for 30 to 35 minutes.

LOKHMA / *This is a delicious creampuff-type batter that is deep-fried and dipped in syrup*

about 50 puffs

SYRUP

2 cups sugar   2 teaspoons lemon juice
1½ cups water

Combine the sugar and water in a saucepan and boil for 10 minutes. Add the lemon juice and boil 1 minute longer. Set aside to cool.

BATTER

1 cup water	*4 eggs*
¼ pound butter	*corn oil*
1 cup flour	

Combine the water and butter in a 2-quart saucepan, and bring the mixture to a boil. Add the flour to the boiling liquid and stir quickly until the dough is smooth and pulls away from the sides of the saucepan. Cool the mixture and beat one egg at a time into the batter until all the eggs have been added, and the dough is smooth. Heat the oil in a deep fryer. Drop ½ teaspoonful of the dough at a time into the hot oil. They will bubble and rise. Turn them occasionally and remove them when they are golden brown. This should take about 5 minutes. Do not overcrowd the fryer. When you have completed cooking the lokhmas, drop them one by one into the cooled syrup, and remove them quickly. Serve within a few hours.

MAMOUNYA / *A nut-filled cookie dipped in syrup*

1½ dozen cookies

FILLING

1 cup walnuts, chopped	*1 teaspoon cinnamon*
2 tablespoons sugar	

Combine the chopped nuts with the sugar and cinnamon and set aside.

SYRUP

2 *cups sugar*	½ *cup chopped walnuts to*
1½ *cups water*	*garnish syrup-coated*
2 *teaspoons lemon juice*	*cookies*

Combine the sugar and water in a saucepan, and cook the mixture for 10 minutes. Add the lemon juice and cook 1 minute longer. Set aside.

PASTRY

1½ *cups flour*	¼ *pound butter*
3 *teaspoons sugar*	¼ *cup water*
1½ *teaspoons baking*	
powder	

Combine the flour, sugar, and baking powder in a mixing bowl. Cut the butter into the flour mixture quickly with your fingers, until it is crumbly. Sprinkle the water over the mixture, and blend it lightly. Gather the dough together into a ball. Cut the dough into 18 pieces, and shape them into balls. Take one ball at a time into your hand, and press your index finger into the center of the ball. Press all around the inside wall to make a round opening. Place a teaspoonful of the filling into the opening and seal it by pushing the opening together. Roll the ball gently in the palm of your hands into the shape of a short cigar. Arrange the pastries on a baking sheet. Brush the top of the pastries with a beaten egg. Bake in a 375° F. oven for 30 to 35 minutes. Dip the hot pastries into the syrup. Remove them when they are thoroughly coated and arrange them in a dish. Sprinkle the syrup-coated pastries with chopped walnuts.

MAMOUL / *Another mouth-watering nut-filled cookie*

2 dozen cookies

FILLING

1½ cups walnuts, finely chopped	*¼ cup sugar*
	1 tablespoon melted butter

Combine the above ingredients in a small bowl and set aside.

PASTRY

1 cup butter	*3 tablespoons milk*
2 tablespoons sugar	*confectioner's sugar*
2 cups flour	

Whip the butter and sugar in a mixing bowl with a beater until they are light and fluffy. Add the flour to the bowl and knead it into the butter and sugar mixture. Sprinkle the milk over the mixture and blend it in lightly. Gather the dough into a ball, and divide it into 24 pieces. Take one piece at a time in your hand, press your index finger into the center of the dough, and press all around the inside to make an opening. Put a teaspoonful of the nut mixture into the opening and seal it gently by pressing the dough together around the filling. Roll it into the shape of an egg or use a mamoul mold. Arrange the mamouls on a baking sheet as you prepare them. Bake the mamouls in a 375° F. oven for 25 or

30 minutes. Remove the pan from the oven and sprinkle the mamouls generously with confectioner's sugar while they are hot.

KARABICH / *Nut-filled cookies made with semolina and whiskey*

15 cookies

FILLING

1 cup walnuts, finely chopped	*1 teaspoon cinnamon*
	¼ cup sugar

Combine the ingredients above in a small bowl and set it aside.

DOUGH

¼ cup sugar	*2¼ teaspoons baking powder*
¼ pound butter, clarified and chilled	*1 tablespoon whiskey*
1 cup flour	*¼ cup water*
1 cup semolina	*½ egg, beaten*
½ teaspoon ground mahleb	

Combine the sugar and the cold butter in a mixing bowl. Beat the mixture with a beater until it is light and fluffy. Add the dry ingredients alternately with the liquids and continue beating until the dough is smooth and well blended. Chill the dough in the refrigerator for 15 minutes.

Take a piece of dough the size of a walnut and roll it into a ball. Hold the ball of dough in your hand and form it into a cone shape. Press your index finger into the center of the cone and press it all around the outside wall to make a cup-shape. Place a teaspoonful of the walnut filling into the opening and seal it gently and securely by pushing the opening together until it is closed. Roll the filled cookie in the palm of your hands as you press it gently into an oval shape. Arrange the karabich on a baking sheet. Continue making the cookies until all of the dough has been used. Bake in a 375° F. oven for 20 to 25 minutes.

Frost each cookie with a teaspoonful of naatiffe.

NAATIFFE / *A fluffy, marshmallowy frosting, flavored with orange-blossom water*

1 pint

¾ cup extra-fine granu- pinch of salt
lated sugar 1 egg white
½ cup orange-flower
water

Combine the sugar and orange-water in a saucepan, and stir over a moderate flame until the sugar is dissolved. When the mixture comes to a boil, lower the flame and let the syrup simmer for 10 minutes, or until it forms a thread when dropped from a spoon.

Add a pinch of salt to the egg white in a bowl. Whip the egg white with a beater until it is stiff and stands in peaks. Pour the hot syrup over the whipped egg white in a very fine stream, beating constantly during the addition of the syrup and afterward until the frosting is stiff and stands in peaks when the beater is lifted. This frosting can be prepared and stored in a covered bowl in the refrigerator for a few days. It is served with mamoul or karabich.

ANOUSHEGHEN

(DESSERTS)

IMRIG HALVAH / *A cereal-like dessert*

4 servings

1 cup sugar	*1 cup Cream of Wheat*
1 cup water	*½ cup pine nuts*
1 cup milk	*cinnamon*
¼ pound sweet butter	

Combine the sugar, water, and milk in a saucepan. Heat the liquid, and stir to dissolve the sugar.

Melt the butter in a saucepan over a low flame. Add the Cream of Wheat and pine nuts. Stir the mixture constantly, until it is lightly browned. Pour the hot liquid over the Cream of Wheat mixture and stir. Cover the saucepan, and lower the flame as much as possible. Simmer until the liquid is absorbed. Remove the saucepan from the stove and replace the cover with a towel to absorb the steam. Stir the halvah from time to time with a fork to break up the lumps, and to separate the grains of Cream of Wheat. Sprinkle with cinnamon. Serve warm.

HALVAH / *A delicious and unusual candy-like dessert*

10 to 12 servings

¾ cup sugar	*½ pound sweet butter*
½ cup heavy cream	*2 cups flour*

Combine the sugar and cream in a bowl, and stir until the sugar is dissolved. Set aside.

Melt the butter in a 10-inch skillet. Add the flour, and stir the mixture over a moderate flame until the butter and flour are well blended. Press down with the back of the spoon, and continue stirring until the mixture is lightly browned. It will take about 30 minutes. Add the sugar and cream mixture, and remove the skillet from the stove. Stir quickly and thoroughly until there are no lumps. Pour the halvah onto a serving plate, smooth the surface, and mark into a diamond pattern with a knife. Serve warm or cold.

BANIROV HALVAH / *Halvah with cheese*

about 12 servings

¾ cup sugar
½ cup cream or milk
½ pound Armenian
cheese or mozzarella

½ cup water
½ pound sweet butter
2 cups flour

Combine the sugar and cream in a bowl, and stir until the sugar is dissolved. Set aside.

Cut the cheese into ½-inch-thick slices, and combine it with the water in a small skillet. Set the skillet over low heat. When the cheese begins to soften on the bottom, turn it to the other side. The cheese should become soft and stringy. Keep it warm until the halvah is ready.

Melt the butter in a 10-inch skillet. Add the flour, and stir the mixture until the butter and flour are well blended, stirring constantly. Over a low flame, press down with the back of the spoon, and stir until the mixture is lightly browned, about 30 minutes. Add the sugar and cream mixture, and remove the skillet from the stove. Stir quickly and thoroughly until there are no lumps. Drain the water from the melted cheese, and add, swirling it lightly through the halvah with a fork. Pour into a serving platter, and smooth the surface. Serve warm.

MUHALLABI / *Rice flour pudding*

5 servings

8 *tablespoons sugar*   *cinnamon to taste*
8 *tablespoons rice flour*   *nuts (optional)*
1 *quart milk*

Combine the sugar, rice flour, and 1 cup of cold milk in a bowl. Stir the mixture with a spoon until it is well blended and smooth. Pour the rest of the milk into a saucepan and place it over a low flame to heat. Gradually add the rice flour mixture to the saucepan, stirring constantly. Continue cooking until the mixture thickens, in just a few minutes. Pour the pudding into individual dessert dishes, and sprinkle the top of each pudding generously with cinnamon. Garnish with shelled pistachios or any other chopped nuts if desired. Serve cold.

GATNABOUR / *Rice pudding*

6 servings

1½ *quarts milk*   8 *tablespoons sugar*
½ *cup rice*

Combine all of the ingredients in a saucepan and bring to a boil. Lower the flame and let the mixture simmer for 45 minutes. Stir frequently. Pour into dessert dishes and chill.

ANOUSHABOUR / *A traditional New Year pudding made of gorgod, fruit, and nuts*

8 to 10 servings

½ cup gorgod	1 cup sugar
7 cups water	1 cup walnut meats
¾ cup dry apricots	½ cup blanched almonds
¾ cup golden raisins	

Combine the gorgod and water in a saucepan. Bring to a boil and set aside to soak overnight.

The next day, cook the gorgod and water over a low flame for 1½ hours. Cut the apricots in half, and add them to the saucepan along with the raisins and sugar. Mix the ingredients and simmer for ½ hour longer.

Place the walnuts and almonds in a baking dish and toast them in a 300° F. oven for 10 minutes.

Save ½ cupful of the nuts to use as a garnish, and stir the balance into the anoushabour. Pour the anoushabour into a deep serving dish and garnish the top with the reserved nuts. Serve cold.

KHUNDSOROV DOLMA / *Baked apple*

6 servings

6 large baking apples	2 teaspoons sugar
½ cup walnuts, coarsely chopped	2 tablespoons butter
½ teaspoon cinnamon	½ cup sugar
	1 cup water

Wash and peel the apples. Remove the stem and core of the apples with a corer and arrange the apples in a baking dish. Combine the walnuts, cinnamon, and 2 teaspoons sugar. Fill the center of the apples with the nut mixture. Place ⅓ of a tablespoon of butter on top of each apple. Dissolve the ½ cup of sugar with 1 cup of water and pour it around the apples. Bake the apples in a 400° F. oven for 1 hour. Baste the apples occasionally with the syrup in the pan while baking. Serve cold.

banir, soorj, yevaylen

(MISCELLANEOUS)

MADZOON / *Madzoon is the Armenian name for yoghurt. Madzoon (or yoghurt) is a bacterial culture. One must put a seeding of the bacteria into warm milk to start a new growth of the culture or madzoon. If the starter is added to hot milk the heat will kill the bacteria, and if it is added to cold milk the bacteria will not grow. Therefore it is very important to add the starter at the right temperature.*

8 servings

1 quart milk
½ pint heavy cream
¼ cup madzoon (If you don't have any on hand, it can be purchased at any supermarket. Always save ¼ cup to use as a starter.)

Pour the milk and cream into a saucepan, and bring them to a boil. Lower the flame before the milk runs over, and simmer on a very low flame for 15 minutes. Pour into a bowl and set aside to cool. Test the temperature of the milk from time to time with your finger: the temperature should be warmer than lukewarm, but not too hot (about 120° F.). Stir the madzoon starter with a spoon until it is smooth, and dilute it with some of the warm milk. Pour this mixture into the warm milk and stir well. Place a plate on the bowl for a cover, and cover the bowl with a large towel to keep the milk warm. Let it rest for 4 hours. Uncover the bowl, and place it in the refrigerator overnight before serving.

TAN / *The Armenian version of buttermilk*

4 servings

2 *cups madzoon*   2 *cups water*

Stir the madzoon with a spoon until it is smooth, and gradually add the water. This is a very refreshing drink served icy cold with many Armenian dishes on hot summer days.

BANIR / *Armenian cheese*

1½ pounds cheese

3½ *quarts milk*   2 *rennet tablets*
1 *pint heavy cream*

Combine the milk and cream in a saucepan. Heat the mixture just enough to be able to hold your finger in the milk without its feeling too hot. Remove the saucepan from the stove. Dissolve the rennet tablets in a small bowl by adding ½ cup of the hot milk. Pour the dissolved mixture into the saucepan and stir thoroughly. Set aside to rest for 12 minutes. Stir the mixture well again. Let it rest again for 10 minutes longer and stir again. Place a cheesecloth bag in a colander. Pour the mixture into the bag slowly. Squeeze the bag gently to help the whey drain out. Place a saucer over the bag and place a heavy object on it, allowing it to drain for about 4 hours. Remove the cheese from the bag. Cut the cheese into 3- or 4-inch pieces and sprinkle them lightly with salt.

DABGADZ BASTEGH / *Fried bastegh and egg*

4 servings

1 egg   *butter*
¼ pound bastegh

Beat the egg lightly. Cut the pieces of bastegh in half, and dip them into the beaten egg to coat both sides. Put 2 tablespoons butter in a skillet and add the pieces of egg-dipped bastegh. Cook the bastegh a minute or so on each side over a moderate flame, and remove to a serving plate. Continue cooking the balance, adding more butter as needed. Serve hot.

HAVGITOV SOUDJOOKH / *Soudjookh and eggs*

4 servings

½ pound soudjookh   *8 eggs*
2 tablespoons butter

Remove the casing on the soudjookh by cutting one end with a knife, and peel it off. Cut the soudjookh into ¼-inch slices.

Put one fourth of the sliced soudjookh into a skillet with ½ tablespoon butter for each serving. Cook over a low flame until the pieces of soudjookh begin to sizzle. Turn them over and break 2 eggs over them. Cook until the eggs are set. Serve immediately. Continue cooking the balance of the soudjookh and eggs.

HAVGITOV PASTERMA / *Pasterma and eggs*

4 servings

2 tablespoons butter   *8 eggs*
¼ pound pasterma, thinly
  sliced

Melt ½ tablespoon of butter in a skillet, and add 5 to 6 slices of pasterma for each serving. Cook over a low flame for a minute, and turn the pasterma over. Break 2 eggs over the pasterma, and cook until they are set sunny side up. Serve immediately. Continue cooking the balance of the pasterma and eggs.

TUTUMOV RECHEL / *A delicious candy-like preserve made with pumpkin*

2 quarts

6 pounds pumpkin (ask for the variety called cheese pumpkin)

1 small bottle lime (11½ grams) to be purchased in a drugstore

water
10 cups sugar
2 sticks of cinnamon
8 cloves
juice of 1 lemon

Cut the pumpkin into ¼-inch slices. Remove the seeds and the skin. Cut each slice into 3-inch pieces.

Dissolve the lime in a gallon of water in a large bowl. Add the pumpkin pieces to the bowl and let them soak in the lime-water overnight. The following day drain the pumpkin, wash the pieces in cold running water, and drain again.

Combine the sugar with 5 quarts of water in a large pot. Bring the mixture to a boil, add the pumpkin, and cook for 3 hours. Add the cinnamon and cloves and continue cooking for 30 minutes. Add the lemon juice and continue cooking for another 30 minutes or until the syrup is thick and the pumpkin is clear. Pour the preserve into sterilized glass jars and store in the refrigerator.

FEESHNEYOV ANOUSH / *Sour cherry preserve*

3 pints

5 *cups sour cherries*   petals *of 3 fragrant roses*
5 *cups sugar*

Wash the cherries and remove the stems. The cherry pits can be removed very easily with a hairpin. Stick the round end of the hairpin into the stem end of the cherry. Push the pin around the pit and slip it out.

Combine the sugar, pitted cherries, and the washed rose petals in a saucepan. Bring the mixture to a boil and stir it. Cook the mixture over a fairly high flame, stirring and watching the pot carefully to be sure it doesn't run over. Cook the cherries for 30 minutes and pour them into 3 sterilized pint-size jars. Seal the jars and refrigerate.

KHOSHOP / *A refreshing cherry drink*

4 servings

2 *cups sour cherries, pitted*   ¾ *cup sugar*
4 *cups water*

Wash the cherries and remove the stems and pits (see recipe above).

Combine the pitted cherries, water, and sugar in a saucepan and cook for 10 minutes. Chill. Serve in glasses as a refreshing drink or in small bowls as a dessert.

SOORJ / *Armenian coffee*

3 servings

6 teaspoons pulverized cof-   6 teaspoons sugar
fee   1 cup water

Combine the above ingredients in a jezveh or any small saucepan. Stir the ingredients and place the pot over a moderate flame. Bring the coffee to a boil three times. Remove the pot from the flame each time before it spills over. Divide the foam from the top of the coffee equally among the demitasse cups and then pour in the coffee. Serve immediately.

RAKI

Raki is the official alcoholic drink of Armenia. It can be found in many specialty liquor stores in cities where there are a large number of Armenian people.

Raki is made with raisins and flavored with anise. It turns milky when served on the rocks. It is good to have at parties with meza or to cure what ails you.

BREAKFAST

Melon
Cheese and olives
Soudjookh and eggs
Coffee or tea

Grapefruit
Katah
Cheese and olives
Coffee or tea

Orange juice
Bastegh and eggs
Bishi
Coffee or tea

MEZA

Midia dolma
Boerag
Hummos

Vospov kheyma
Tourshi
Adjeh
Yalanchi dolma

Topik
Dabgadz patlijan
Ooghegh
Kimionov kufta

LUNCHEON

Izmir kufta
Salata
Fresh fruit
Coffee

Khavourma wrapped in soft
    lavash
Jajukh
Fruit compote
Tea

Gelorig
Raw green vegetables
Khundsorov dolma
Tea

DINNER

Tan abour
Kufta
Fassoulia salata
Bourma
Coffee or tea

Jajukh
Lahmajoon
Baba ghanoush
Khourabia
Coffee or tea

Turlu guevej
Prinzov pilaf
Jevisli
Coffee or tea

Shish kebab
Bulghour pilaf
Salata
Tan
Lavash
Revani
Coffee or tea

Jigerr
Vospov piaz
Raw vegetables
Khundsorov dolma
Coffee or tea

Fish plaki
Porov hav
String bean stew
Salata
Pakhlava
Coffee or tea

Khabourgha
Havgitov spanakh
Salata
Karabich
Coffee or tea

Lule kebab
Bamiya
Bulghour pilaf
Lokhma
Coffee or tea

Lahana dolma
Madzoon
Tomatesov salata
Imrig halvah
Coffee or tea

Keshkeg
Tourshi
Salata
Kadayif
Coffee or tea

Shishboereg
Duezmah
Salata
Gatnabour
Coffee or tea

Patlijan karni yarek
Prinzov pilaf
Salata
Halvah
Coffee or tea

BOSTON

Euphrates Grocery
101 Shawmut Avenue
Boston, Massachusetts 02118

Syrian Grocery Importing Company
270 Shawmut Avenue
Boston, Massachusetts 02118

CHICAGO

Columbus Food Market
2604 West Lawrence Avenue
Chicago, Illinois 60625

DALLAS

Purity Importing Company
4507 Swiss Avenue
Dallas, Texas 75204

LOS ANGELES

Bezjian's Grocery
4725 Santa Monica Boulevard
Los Angeles, California 90029

C & K Import Company
2771 West Pico Boulevard
Los Angeles, California 90006

NEW ORLEANS

Central Grocery Company
923 Decatur Street
New Orleans, Louisiana 70116

NEW YORK

House of Yemen East
370 Third Avenue
New York, New York 10016

K. Kalustyan
123 Lexington Avenue
New York, New York 10016

Kassos Brothers
570 Ninth Avenue
New York, New York 10036

Karnig Tashjian
380 Third Avenue
New York, New York 10016

SAN FRANCISCO

Istanbul Pastries
247 Third Street
San Francisco, California 94103

Persian Imports
347 Grant Avenue
San Francisco, California 94108

WASHINGTON, D.C.

Aloupis Company
916 Ninth Street N.W.
Washington, D.C. 20001

Skenderis Greek Imports
1612 Twentieth Street N.W.
Washington, D.C. 20009

index

RACHEL (NÉE ANSOORIAN) HOGROGIAN was born on the island of Cypress, where her parents had emigrated from their native city of Aintab, Turkey. Like many Armenians who were forced to leave their homes in what was once Armenia, her family could bring little with them but their love and preservation of the region's food, music, and history.

Mrs. Hogrogian's husband is from the city of Erzinjan, and although the book is a well-balanced cookbook, Mrs. Hogrogian has included a few special dishes from Aintab and Erzinjan. The lahmajoon made by the Aintabtsees (people of Aintab) is unsurpassable, as you will see by her recipe, and you have never tasted keshkeg as good as the keshkeg from Erzinjan which she has included here.

Rachel Hogrogian has two daughters who are delighted to have recorded finally the recipes of their favorite dishes, and two grandchildren who enjoy testing them.

NONNY HOGROGIAN, one of the daughters of Rachel Hogrogian, is well known as a designer and illustrator of books for children. In 1966 she won the Caldecott medal for the year's "most distinguished American picture book for children," awarded for her illustrations for *Always Room for One More* by Sorche Nic Leodhas.